Angels

PLEASE HEAR ME

JENNY SMEDLEY

HAY HOUSE

Australia • Canada • Hong Kong • India
South Africa • United Kingdom • United States

First published and distributed in the United Kingdom by:

Hay House UK Ltd, 292B Kensal Rd, London W10 5BE. Tel.: (44) 20 8962 1230; Fax: (44) 20 8962 1239. www.hayhouse.co.uk

Published and distributed in the United States of America by:

Hay House, Inc., PO Box 5100, Carlsbad, CA 92018-5100. Tel.: (1) 760 431 7695 or (800) 654 5126; Fax: (1) 760 431 6948 or (800) 650 5115. www.hayhouse.com

Published and distributed in Australia by:

Hay House Australia Ltd, 18/36 Ralph St, Alexandria NSW 2015. Tel.: (61) 2 9669 4299; Fax: (61) 2 9669 4144. www.hayhouse.com.au

Published and distributed in the Republic of South Africa by:

Hay House SA (Pty), Ltd, PO Box 990, Witkoppen 2068. Tel./Fax: (27) 11 467 8904. www.hayhouse.co.za

Published and distributed in India by:

Hay House Publishers India, Muskaan Complex, Plot No.3, B-2, Vasant Kunj, New Delhi – 110 070. Tel.: (91) 11 4176 1620; Fax: (91) 11 4176 1630. www.hayhouse.co.in

Distributed in Canada by:

Raincoast, 9050 Shaughnessy St, Vancouver, BC V6P 6E5. Tel.: (1) 604 323 7100; Fax: (1) 604 323 2600

A catalogue record for this book is available from the British Library.

ISBN 978-1-84850-288-8

Printed and bound in Great Britain by CPI Bookmarque, Croydon CR0 4TD.

All of the papers used in this product are recyclable, and made from wood grown in managed, sustainable forests and manufactured at mills certified to ISO 14001 and/or EMAS.

Dedication

As always, I'd like to thank Hay House for continuing to have confidence in me and for giving me the opportunity to fulfil my life path as a seed-planter.

My much loved husband Tony has been, as always, my sounding board, and he deserves a lot of credit for the part he plays both in my life and in my writing.

I'd also like to thank all the wonderful people who have shared their inspirational stories with us on these pages.

Angels come in all shapes and sizes, and often appear where you least expect them, so try to always walk in the light of angel energy and you'll always be ready to meet them –
Jenny Smedley

About the Author

Based in the beautiful county of Somerset in the UK, and happily married for over 40 years, Jenny Smedley DPLT is a qualified past-life regressionist, author, TV and radio presenter and guest, international columnist and spiritual consultant specializing in the subjects of past lives and angels. She's also an animal intuitive and tree communicator. She lives with her husband, Tony, a spiritual healer, and her reincarnated Springador dog, KC.

Her own current life was turned around by a vision from one of her past lives, in which she knew the man known today as Garth Brooks, and problems and issues related to that life were healed and resolved in a few seconds. For two years she hosted her own spiritual chat show on Taunton TV, interviewing people such as David Icke, Reg Presley, Uri Geller and Diana Cooper. Jenny has appeared on many TV shows in the UK, USA, Ireland and Australia, including *The Big Breakfast*, *Kelly*, *Open House*, *The Heaven and Earth Show*, *Kilroy* and *Jane Goldman Investigates*. She has also been a guest on hundreds of radio shows including *The Steve Wright Show* on BBC Radio 2 and *The Richard Bacon Show* on BBC Five Live in the UK, as well as in places as far-flung as Australia, New Zealand, Iceland, Tasmania, South Africa, the USA and the Caribbean.

Her most recent press appearances in the UK:

The Daily Mail –
'World Renowned'

The Daily Express –
'Unique rapport with the natural world'

The Sunday Times Style Magazine –
'A global phenomenon'

After being shown her Master Path by an angel, Jenny was given the ability to create Mirror Angel Portraits and remote aura pictures, and to help others connect to their angels. Her website is: www.jennysmedley.com.

Contents

Foreword

As a journalist, you have this wonderful ticket into a world where it's OK to be nosy. Essentially, you pry into the corners of peoples' lives and distil and relay the information in interesting ways to the readers of whatever publication you write for. I am lucky that most of my work has been with people who fascinate me or with whom I consider it a privilege to converse. In light of what I am doing now it was an incredibly lucky day when I rang Jenny Smedley to interview her about her book *Soul Angels*. I had read the book and my God had it resonated with me. Within a week of finishing it I was off to a past-life regressionist mentioned at the back of the book and what I did over the course of 24 hours in Cottage Retreat made my life change rapidly. Things that had dragged me down for so long that it was as if they had become an intrinsic a part of me, disappeared. The fog left my mind and good things came in ripples, a pleasant phone call here, a little bonus there, small things, then, *Boom*: Love, Ambition, Energy and finally Connection started to flow through my veins.

My life is different now in more ways than I could have imagined and I don't know where I will be by the time this is published, but I know that amid the normal ups and downs, fluctuations, I will be on the whole happier, less lonely and less disconnected. All that is in this book resonates with something deep inside me. A part of me I have not yet clearly met but one that flows to the surface in beautifully connected moments. A wonderful walk outside in the fresh country air or by the sea, a lovely meal with my family, a passionate kiss, that calm moment just before I slip off to sleep or when I dream deep in meditation are all peaceful moments when I really seem to get *it*.

I read this book in manuscript form with a near constant bubble of something, excitement maybe, bouncing in my stomach. I can't see energy and, more and more, it's frustrating me, but I can slowly start to sense it. There is powerful energy coming from this book and at times it became simply too much and I needed to zone out. I'd put it aside and focus on something else. But after a few days I would pick it up, feel the energy bounce inside once again, breathe deep and allow myself to sit back and take it in.

I'm as confused at times as anyone by my day-to-day existence on Earth. The relationships I form, both good and bad, the heartbreak I have felt, the depression that seeps slowly into me, the poverty, the downright wrong that exists in the world and the things that just don't work out despite my best intentions all make me feel powerless and simply sad. One thing I have learned is that we should never take things at face value, that the bigger picture is always at work and we need to read, we need to keep wanting to understand and learn more about life and spirituality, and finding our purpose. Life is a baffling process of mere existence without the tools and knowledge that people like Jenny provide, and therefore I would encourage anyone and everyone to read as much as they can from the wealth of divine wisdom that is now so readily available.

I am lucky that I have led a relatively charmed life to date. Aside from my personal ups and downs there has been little that would be considered traumatic. Moving forward, I know at some stage inevitabilities such as death, the challenges of marriage and maybe parenting will cross my path, but now I am not afraid or overwhelmed. There is a passage in the Bible, Psalm 23:4 – 'Even though I walk through the valley of the shadow of death, I will fear no evil, for you are with me. Your rod and your staff, they comfort me.' I have always loved it. It stuck in my mind immediately on first reading it, and I mull over it from time to time.

I previously thought it was referring to another part of me, in the 'you' that is by my side part, and perhaps it is a phrase laden with many meanings, but now, for me, I like to think of it referring to millions of energies, angels, always at our side as we walk through the valley of the shadow of death, doubt, darkness and tough times.

'Death' is a word layered with meaning but most importantly to me it portrays an extinguished candle inside. Lack of connection, no sense of purpose and self-doubt extinguish this candle that wants to glow inside us all. Even though we may do things we doubt, continuously ignoring our instincts, angels will be there to help us. It is one of the most truly loving relationships we shall ever experience, and even though we may fail repeatedly, ignore the whispers on our shoulders, banish those feelings in our gut telling us not to do something and brashly do it anyway, we will still be loved and we are never abandoned, ever.

Even though we may not understand why bad things seemingly happen to us, why people let us down and why hardship exists, someone is at our side; knowing what Jenny conveys in this book, we should never be afraid. As we grow and begin to listen more to ourselves and our angels, the angels shall proudly be at our sides, smiling. Maybe then when life is beautiful we shall be able to see them more clearly.

This book takes the fear out of making mistakes and it shows us the light. It helps us weather the hardships that life throws at us seemingly randomly to toughen us up. Most importantly, it makes us realize in our darkest and most confusing moments that there is design beneath the disorder and angels holding our hands, whispering lovely thoughts and trying desperately to help us, and it gives us tools to hear them. Enjoy this book. I really did. Welcome its wisdom into your life.

– Holly White, writer and presenter
www.holly.ie

Preface

You never know when something extraordinary is going to happen, and whether, when it does, it will be a good or a bad thing. Certainly, that day when we'd set off from home, we'd felt safe and secure in our big, comfy car, a recent purchase. It gave us a good feeling always knowing that our car had many safety features, including lots of different airbags, side-impact protection and a roll cage. We didn't know it at the time, but a few minutes later we were going to need a lot more than airbags to save us. We were going into the nearest town, and Tony was driving, with me as passenger. We drove along the quiet back streets, on our way to do the weekly shop. We came around a bend and suddenly saw something surreal and quite terrifying.

A car was flying through the air on the other side of the road, coming in our direction. As it hurtled aloft, it bounced off a parked car, which threw it right onto our side of the road, still airborne. For a split millisecond we could clearly see the car's underside as it rolled in mid-air, its exhaust pipe still puffing grey smoke. On its current trajectory it was certain that it would either land on top of our car, or, at best, it would slam into the road a couple of feet away and then, because it was coming at us down a steep hill, it would hurtle and catapult along the road and barrel into our bonnet, and all one-and-a-half tons of its distorted metal would come through our windscreen. No amount of airbags would save us if that mighty weight landed smack on top of us either from above or in front. All we had time to do, literally, was say, 'Oh,' and it was all over.

You never expect it to happen to you. You never really expect such a devastating accident. Nevertheless, that morning my husband Tony had done his usual ritual, wrapping our car in a bubble of white light, like armour. I'd always left this to Tony as he was particularly good at it, and he never forgot to do it. It's one of the many things I rely on him for, and I have no doubt that on this occasion his connection to angelic power saved our lives.

Our car stopped as Tony stood on the brakes. We had no time to think. No time for our lives to flash before our eyes, no time to pray, no time to scream for help from our angels. I suppose this is how sudden death often comes, not with a yell but with a double 'Oh.'

The motor of the flying car was still running, so of course fuel was still flowing, and it was pouring out of the upside-down engine. It crossed my mind briefly to wonder if the car would explode in flames as it slammed into us. No amount of award-winning safety devices would save us if we were crushed from above and then burned.

And then it was as if the flying car hit an invisible brick wall in mid-air. It slammed down onto the road, never completing its arc. It landed on its own roof, and started the seemingly inevitable, fast-speed slide toward us. Then it suddenly twisted, as if shoved by a mighty hand, and one corner lodged against the kerbstones, bringing the whole thing to a sudden and unexpected halt a few feet from us. We sat for a few seconds, in shock, noticing that the crashed car *still* had its engine running. Then we both jumped out and went to help the passengers. As Tony jumped out of our car, he had his mobile phone in his hand, already dialling 999. He told me later he'd thought that maybe he'd have to call the Fire Brigade as well as an ambulance because, as we were now parked downhill from the car and its leaking fuel tank, he thought petrol might stream down the road and still set our car on fire. But, bizarrely, the dribble of petrol just vanished, evaporated instantly, as if it had never been.

Later, the driver of the car that had pretensions to be an aeroplane admitted to all and sundry that she'd been trying to change a cassette tape at the time of the crash, and had been looking down, distracted. She said she never even saw the parked cars and wasn't aware immediately after the accident that she'd hit anything. Afterwards, with the statements of several eyewitnesses, it became clear that the first one she'd hit had acted like a ski-ramp, lifting her car skywards and turning it turtle. Her vehicle had then bounced off the next car's bonnet, and that had flipped it over onto the other side of the road and into our path.

The driver was the only person in the car. The roof had been squashed by the impact and the driver, unhurt, just bewildered, was struggling to crawl out through the smashed window on the passenger side. She refused to stay put, despite a well-meaning first-aider saying she should, and grabbed my hand to help her get out, insisting that she was unhurt, although she was bleeding. Tony had called for an ambulance and the police arrived, too. It was a miracle that no one was seriously hurt, no one had been crushed by the falling car, and it hadn't crashed down on top of us. As you can imagine, I was very pleased that Tony had done the morning ritual before we'd left home, otherwise I might well not be writing this!

Tony stayed at the scene of the accident to give a statement to the police at the request of the paramedics, and I took our car on to do the shopping, so that we wouldn't miss a later appointment – driving very carefully, I might say. This happened a few weeks ago as I write, and during the following week I kept getting messages in my mind to 'go slower'. I can be a bit of a speed merchant generally, as I'm always in a hurry to get where I'm going. So I thought perhaps these thoughts were just leftovers from the shock of our near miss. Even if that were so, I still decided to obey them, telling Tony the reason why I was driving slower than usual.

People often ask me how to tell the difference between a genuine warning from angels and just random thoughts. I always feel that if it's just a quick sentence and the meaning can't in any way be misunderstood or misinterpreted, such as 'go slower', then it is for real. This sort of thing is going to be a definite warning. Strange, confusing messages, or clipped-off sentences and garbled words, however, can be one of several things. They can be random thoughts, of course, like daydreaming, but more often they are our intuition, and the latent psychic ability we all have, 'overhearing' in our minds someone else in the neighbourhood's thoughts or conversations. I have confirmation of this because when we lived in a town I used to get a lot of them, but now that we've moved back out into the countryside and don't have so many near neighbours, I don't get so many of these 'eavesdropping' thoughts. Or they can be part one of a cryptic message from your angel. You're meant to make a note of them in this case, and gradually over time your 'angel diary' will come to make sense, and you'll understand what they were about.

Anyway, back to my warning to go slower. Yesterday (as I write) I was en route to the hairdresser's about 12 miles from home. I was driving slowly – after all, I'd been told to, and you don't ignore things like that if you have any sense. I had reached a place on the journey where I'd normally have been in fifth gear and travelling at about 60mph, but because of the warning ringing in my mind, I was still in fourth gear and only doing about 35mph.

Suddenly the car started to make a horrendous noise from the back end. Its handling wasn't compromised, and at first I thought the noise was coming from another vehicle. Then I thought that perhaps it was the strong cross-wind buffeting the car and making a noise. Then, deciding it was none of these things, I stopped the car. The nearside rear tyre was completely blown, shredded and split, as if it had exploded. I'd never had any kind of a puncture before and had always expected that if I did, the car would slew all over the road and possibly end up hitting something else. But nothing like that had happened. However, when I got to the garage, the mechanic told me that if I'd been travelling at any speed, the outcome could have been very serious, and I could easily have had an accident.

You might ask why didn't the angels, if indeed it was

them that warned me, stop the puncture happening? There's always an answer to these questions if you look deeply enough. If I'd never had the puncture I would have continued to my destination. As it was, I had to wait for help and then drive into a different town to the tyre-fitters to replace the 'space-saving' tyre that modern cars carry as a temporary spare. I also had to call the hairdresser's and apologize that I wasn't going to make my appointment. The story didn't end there, and the reason for the puncture happening at all was explained. I was not meant to go to that location on that day at that time. As I said, the town where the hairdresser's was, and the place I should have gone to, was a different town to the one I ended up in to get the new tyre, but a road ran directly between the two towns, linking them. While I was waiting for the tyre to be fitted, at one end of the road between the towns a stream of police cars, fire engines and ambulances went up toward the town where the hairdresser's was. It became obvious that a very big accident had occurred up the road, and was along the very stretch I'd have been on if I'd not had the puncture and had gone the 'right' way. That day was not my time to die or be seriously hurt, and so I was prevented from being on that stretch of road.

I've told you these two incidents to demonstrate two things. First, they show the importance of asking for angelic protection, and second, to listen when help is offered. But, you are possibly saying, 'I do ask!' 'I do listen!' 'I just never get an answer!' You have most likely noted that some people, especially the rich and famous, seem to do quite nicely, thank you, even though they might say they don't even believe in angels, and yet there you are, a total believer, *desperate* to communicate with them, trying all the time to get them to help you, and you get nothing. If angels love us all and if we can all get help from them, you might ask, then why is it that some people seem blessed and others seem ignored? Some of the most successful people in the world don't even seem to believe in angels enough to ask them for help, and yet they still seem to get it. Others are desperate to be heard and yet their prayers go unanswered. Why is this? How can we change it? The reasons for this, and the answers as to how to change things, are why I wrote this book, and as you read on through the chapters, you will find answers to your questions.

Angel experiences aren't always action-packed and filled with potential danger. In fact, most times they are very beautiful. Recently I had a very strange and quite magical experience involving a phenomenon that I'd never heard of before, but afterwards I was able to find several documented accounts of others who'd experienced the same thing. I was fast asleep one night. Bear in mind that I live in a very small village and it's very quiet, especially at night. All you can normally hear if you're out in the night is the calls of owls and an occasional fox barking in the distance. This night something woke me. I never knew what, but as I lay there, I realized I could hear an incredibly beautiful voice singing very quietly. As I listened, transfixed, the voice seemed to come closer, and the purity of the notes would have been envied even by the likes of Susan Boyle. The voice rose and fell, and the high notes were unbelievably clear. Then, just as I was wondering what on Earth I was listening to, other voices joined in, just as beautiful as the first. The thought that crossed my mind was that a choir of angels must be in the front garden, just feet from the window. I got out of bed and crossed to the window. I pulled the curtains a little apart and stared out into the starlit night. The front garden was lit up almost as bright as day, but there was absolutely no one there. There was no wind, and the night was still and silent, apart from the crystalline voices. And then it hit me, and I knew with total certainty that I was listening to the voices of angels. Why they came I don't know, but they filled me with joy and wonder. I got back into bed and they sang me back to sleep. In the morning I was still awestruck at the incredible exquisiteness of what I'd heard. As I said, I've discovered that hearing a 'choir of angels' is an experience shared by a few others. I feel very privileged to have heard it.

Introduction

There are many unhappy people in the world, and it's sometimes frustrating to see really wonderful souls going through life unfulfilled, depressed even, when they have so much to offer and so much potential. Of course, as a believer in reincarnation, having had its existence proved to me over and over again, I know that they'll have another chance to shine and enjoy a fulfilling life, as many chances as they need in fact, and that this current life isn't the be all and end all of their soul's journey.

But that's not much consolation to them in their present situation.

In my work as a magazine columnist I have hundreds of people writing to me in the hopes of finding a solution to their worries, and looking for helpful advice from an intuitive perspective. There are many reasons for their unhappiness, and sometimes they've despaired, losing faith in angels and in ever attaining a better way of living. Some people yearn for a true and meaningful relationship, but it always seems to escape them. Some people feel very alone and unsupported and don't know how to reach out for help. Some people are hard up and believe they'd be happy if they didn't have to struggle so much. Some people are suffering debilitating conditions or regular pain and don't know how to cope. When they lose faith in their angels' ability or willingness to help them, they come close to giving up and sink into negative emotions.

The problem is that their fate then becomes a self-fulfilling prophecy, as their energy enters a downward spiral from which they can't escape. Negative emotions create negative energy, and that in turn naturally attracts negative outcomes just like some sort of nasty magnet. When people start to feel they have no power and no control over their destinies, and believe their lives are never going to get better, they become afraid of the future. There's no reason for them to be afraid, because a connection to angels will not only provide solutions to many of the problems they face, it will also give them a lifeline to grasp that will enable them to move out of the darkness and into the light, and thereby regain a grip on their own fate.

Resolving their issues in a practical way won't necessarily make the person happy, or at least not permanently. There are many married, gregarious, rich, healthy people who are still unhappy despite their apparent success and good fortune. Angels can help them find the true key to a genuinely happy state of soul that doesn't depend on anyone or anything else.

Before I started work on this book I conducted an internet survey because I wanted to have a firm idea of how people felt about angels and the impact angels could have on their lives, and was delighted, if a little surprised, to see that:

- **92.9 per cent of people who filled in the survey answers do believe in angels.**

- **64.3 per cent believe they have communicated with an angel.**

- **100 per cent of the people who took part believe the world would be a better place if everyone believed in angels – and they are right!**

This was very encouraging.

The people who do believe in angels all want help from them. Some of them have had it, but many have difficulty connecting with their angels, and seem to think they never will. But there *is* hope. They *can* be heard by angels. It's all down to having the right energy. Angels exist in another dimension to us. They can't naturally be in our dimension and we can't naturally be in theirs, because each dimension has a different rate of vibration. Every living thing, and even every inanimate thing, vibrates or pulses, including the very planet we walk on, but our human vibration is much slower than that of angels. This is because we are 'earthbound' and have to live in balance, physically with the Earth, which has a slower rate of vibration than the dimension in which angels exist. The only way to raise our vibration enough to be able to reach the angelic dimension and ask for help is energetically, on a soul level, by generating overwhelmingly positive energy, which also means calm energy.

This book is written mostly for all those people who have difficultly in maintaining the right energy state. It's to show the forlorn that, no matter how desperate their plight appears, it's not too late, there is a helping hand reaching down to them, and it is possible for them to grasp their destiny and take charge of their own lives and their own reality. It's to help them to see that angels are the greatest levellers of all, and love *each and every one of us* exactly the same amount. I want to help people in need to connect with their angels and to get the help they need to finally grasp what they've been searching for all their lives.

CHAPTER 1

The Right Kind of Energy

The right kind of energy is smooth like melted honey. It has no lumps and no jagged edges, and like honey it's sweet and easy to mould. Because this sort of energy automatically raises the vibration of the person it's attached to, it makes it easier for angels to connect with that person. Then, because this kind of energy is pliable, it makes it easy for angels to take hold of it and reshape it so as to change that person's reality for them. On the other hand, if the energy is the wrong sort, it'll be prickly and unyielding like a cactus plant, which will slow the person's vibrations and make the angels unable to get too close to that person. Because this kind of energy is rigid and hard, angels can't grasp it and form it into something better for the person with whom it's associated, no matter how desperately help might be wanted.

Some people naturally have the right energy to get help, even unsolicited help, from angels, because they're confident – and confidence is one of the things that creates smooth energy. Without your energy being right, you have no chance of an angel intervening on your behalf, because they simply can't interact with you. So *you have to stop doubting yourself.* You have to stop seeing others as being better or more deserving than you. Your angel *loves you*, and the more you believe that, the smoother your energy will become and the more easily you'll receive angelic help. Have confidence in your angel's love for you. Remember that your angel exists *because* of you only, *for* you only and wants nothing more than to bring you the happiness you deserve.

'LUCKY' PEOPLE

If someone's meant to have good things happen in their life, possibly to enable them to fulfil some unfinished business from a past life, or because the beneficial situation is necessary for their soul's development, then, so long as they have the right energy, their angels can step in, even if they haven't actually been asked, to help them achieve their rightful destiny. These kinds of people will be literally drenched in the right kind of energy to enable angels to reach them and to help them, and even if they profess not to believe in angels, it will make no difference. These people will appear to be 'lucky'. The reason they appear so is that their lives and minds have been filled from the word 'go' by naturally positive emotions and affirmations.

These emotions and affirmations can be any of the following – what I call assertive positive emotional states:

- **lovingness**
- **serenity**
- **trust**
- **happiness**
- **confidence**
- **awe**
- **optimism**
- **patience.**

Assertive, positive emotions create apparently serene yet dynamic and powerful energy. This energy is absolutely perfect for enlisting angelic help. Angels can virtually bathe in this kind of energy, get very close to the person emitting it and step in with dramatic help when it's needed, even without being asked.

Now, some people may tell you that angels can't help unless they're asked, but to me those who have this balanced and powerful kind of energy are inviting help in a way, without even realizing it. Just their heightened vibrations are enough to elicit an angelic response. By creating the perfect environment for angels, even unwittingly, they're inviting angels to be in their lives. Also, as I said, they are most likely walking the path they were destined to walk, and so things will appear to fall into place naturally.

These people also have a lot of what I call submissive positive energy states, such as:

- **gratitude**

- **acceptance**

- **humility**

- **compassion**

- **tolerance**

- **amusement**

- **anticipation**

- **sympathy.**

These emotions create stable, balanced, gentle emotion, which again allows angels to stay close. These energy flows can be likened to smooth airflow. Imagine a small airplane that needs refuelling (this is you wanting help from angels). If the air around the plane is even and calm, then the refuelling aircraft (the angel) can come close, safely and easily, and dispense the fuel (the help you need). On the other hand, if the air around the plane is turbulent and bumpy, the refuelling plane won't be able to link up with it.

Angels have some very special ways to rekindle your faith in them, and one device you can use to help them show you these special ways is very simple: smile. Positive energy begets positive energy, and you can multiply its power exponentially with a simple smile. Next time your woes are getting the better of you and someone asks, 'How are you?' just smile and say, 'I'm absolutely great!' I guarantee the person will smile right back at you. Do this all day, and what at first will have been an act on your part, which on its own wouldn't really help you, will soon become the truth. Keep a score of how many smiles you can generate in other people, and give yourself an angel brownie point for every one. At the end of the day think about how you feel and how you made all those other people feel. This might seem like small stuff, but it all adds up, and starts to rebuild your energy.

Sometimes people ask me for help and they just need a little encouragement to get back on track with their angels. In these cases angels will often give me a sign for the person, and when the sign comes true for them, their faith is restored completely.

One such woman was Yvonne, an Australian woman who wrote to me via my *Take 5* column. She wanted to know if she'd find love one day, and if her angel was ever going to help her do so. I asked my angel if I could be given some signs that would come true and thereby help prove to Yvonne that her angels had helped her. I was shown a man behind the wheel of a blue car, accompanied by a dog that glowed so much it appeared to be golden. This man was Yvonne's soulmate and would be coming to her. I told Yvonne what I'd seen, in the column, but also gave her the warning that this would happen in 'heaven's time', so she needed to have faith and be patient. That was in March 2008. Just a few days ago (in July 2010) I got this e-mail from her:

> Dear Jenny
> I'm happy to say that in January this year I met the love of my life, and he had a blue car and a golden dog! Absolutely amazing!

Job done, I think.

A DIFFICULT QUESTION

I was asked by someone recently how I could account for people who are, for instance, killed in disasters such as earthquakes. He asked, 'Surely, some of them will have been filled with positive thoughts prior to the event, and yet they still died, and horribly. Why?'

I'm not saying that positive thinking will get you a perfect life, but that it does help move you along your rightful path. Having positive energy doesn't mean your life will be trouble-free. That's why no one can or should be blamed for having something bad happen to them. Sometimes bad events are just something we're meant to endure and learn from for whatever reason, but if you can maintain positive energy throughout difficult times – which I know is not easy at all – then you'll maintain a connection to your angels, who'll then do everything possible to help you get through the trauma you're facing. If your final time has come and you must die, then a connection with angels will help your passing and fast-track your soul's crossing into spirit.

Many people who took photos of the Twin Towers tragedy found images of angels in them, rising up from the debris, and believe they were carrying the souls of those who died, out and upwards. Some people believe that every one of those souls had an angel waiting to wing them to heaven, and that their deaths had a divine purpose, perhaps to cause a planetary energy shift. Many genuine psychics 'felt' the tragedy happen without being told, because they experienced such a shift in the planet's energy as all those souls left at the same time.

It's a sad fact that some people are destined to die in earthquakes or wars, or accidents or crimes, etc., and that's what will be right for them, for reasons we cannot possibly appreciate in our mortal forms. But in the meantime, getting along the right path is what we all should concentrate on, and being positive about it seems to create the right steps, because that way people have a happier life and achieve what they came here to do.

My own life isn't perfect by any means, and some things are just going to happen to me, positive or not, because my soul's progress depends on them, but negative thinking *can* and *does* create extra negative outcomes, and renders angels unable to change things even if they're things that don't need to happen. Positive thinking helps mitigate the necessary 'bad' stuff and allows angels to change what isn't necessary.

REPRESSING NEGATIVE EMOTIONS

I was also asked recently about the wisdom of always repressing negative emotions, and questioned about the possible health impact of doing such a thing. Well, this person had misunderstood the concept of positive thinking entirely. I'm not talking about *suppressing* negative feelings and emotions. That isn't going to work, because the negative emotions are still in your energy, whether you talk about them or express them in your behaviour or not. The idea is not to have negative thoughts at all, because your thoughts flood through your energy, swamping it and manipulating it, and it's your energy that affects your angel's ability to connect with you, or not. Unfortunately, negative thoughts are what we're often conditioned to have by society today. If just acting well and hiding our thoughts were all it took then everyone would be doing it and everyone would be happy. Angels can't be fooled by Oscar-winning acting ability, because they only see our energy.

This conditioned negative state is very, very difficult to overcome, which is why so many people are still unhappy and unfulfilled, and haven't managed, despite years of trying, to connect with their angels. A person needs to be vigilant and to learn to monitor their every flicker of thought. They need to see each thought as a seed, and before they give it free rein to grow, think what it might grow into, whether good energy or bad. Gradually, with determination and the will to succeed, they will be able to change their old self-destructive patterns.

A GREAT EXAMPLE

My husband Tony is a great example of someone who doesn't give in to negative states of fear, even in situations when fear would be a natural reaction. In stressful situations he literally exudes calmness, and at times it's almost possible for me to see his angels floating around him. For instance, back in 1987 when England was struck by a hurricane, we were woken up in the night by the dreadful sound of the horizontal wind buffeting our cottage. When I looked out of the window I was horrified to see something that looked almost alien, as the landscape was hidden by a maelstrom of leaves and branches, and actual pieces of buildings, whirling around us. I felt a little like Dorothy in *The Wizard of Oz*, and almost expected our cottage to take flight. We had three horses at the time, and when I saw that the stables had been virtually demolished, and only some snapped-off parts of the walls were still standing, my immediate reaction was terror that the horses must have been severely injured, and I felt unable to cope. Tony not only maintained calm energy, but he managed to transfer this energy to me. We went outside, stumbling over uprooted trees and dodging flying pieces of debris, and found that miraculously the horses were standing in the ruins of their stables, quite untouched. Because we were calm we were able to calm them, too, and safely remove them and release them into the safety of the sheltered paddock.

Then, a few years ago, Tony had to face difficult surgery. Again he remained calm in the face of natural fear and apprehension, refusing to become scared. His subsequent recovery from the surgery was so good and so rapid that he totally amazed his doctors. This was a classic example of a bad thing that was meant to happen and yet was able to be endured with the minimum of suffering.

MOST IMPORTANT FACT

Always remember that happiness might not come from the direction you're expecting. Always ask your angels for happiness, rather than what *you* think will make you happy. Otherwise you could end up with all your dreams seeming to come true, but in reality ending up being rich, alone and sad.

Angels know best!

CHAPTER 2

The Wrong Kind of Energy

Desperate energy has the wrong wavelength to be accessed by the angels. This energy state slows down a person's vibration, and it's why the more desperate someone becomes to connect with their angels, the harder it becomes to achieve that connection.

Aggressive negative energy states include:

- greed
- fear
- envy
- hatred
- anger
- depression
- grief

- **despair**

- **distrust**

- **cruelty**

- **violence**

- **shame**

- **humiliation**

- **contempt**

- **desperation**

- **impatience.**

You'll notice that there are a lot more of these kinds of aggressively negative emotions than there were of the positive, and this just goes to show why it's so difficult to avoid them.

MONEY ISSUES

Problems that generate these kinds of negative emotions obviously also generate negative energy, driving a wedge between people and the angels from whom they so desperately want to get help. Sometimes people might seem to get what they want despite having these kinds of emotions, but they don't always get what they *need*.

A classic example of the kind of feeling which can get the wrong result was demonstrated to my husband Tony one evening recently. He was in a small supermarket, the 'open all hours' kind of thing, and the moment was approaching of the National Lottery cut-off time for buying tickets. Apparently the machine down the road in another shop had broken down, so people were flooding into this shop to buy their tickets. There was, Tony said, a sense of building panic as the time ticked by and the queue for tickets lengthened. Apparently at the moment of cut-off the computers just shut down, so there could be no extra time allowed. Tony said the people queuing became more and more distraught, even to the point of being near tears. Some of them got very aggressive as they saw their chances vanishing along with the minutes. This sort of dependency on money as the key to all happiness will actually push angels away, and if these people do ever win some money, they're likely to find that in the end, after their initial euphoria, the money becomes a bit of a letdown, because their spirit won't be fed by it, and it's their spirit that is really hungry rather than their wallet.

Sometimes the greatest gift an angel can give you is to *not* answer your prayers.

I recently met a man, whom I'll call George for the sake of his privacy, who told me that he'd been a heroin addict for quite a few years. All he thought he wanted in life was enough cash to 'score' whenever he wanted to, to buy a fast car and to entice a girlfriend who would take care of him and get high with him. He got the cash, the car and the girl, but these were all things he wanted, not needed, and his angel knew better. Inside, his soul was crying out. He hated how his parents broke down and cried when they saw his addiction, but he didn't know how to stop. He hated the way people looked at him with condemnation in their eyes. He hated the deep hunger he felt, but didn't know how to appease. He hated the scars on his arms that were caused by collapsed veins, and showed everyone what he was, and he often thought of getting a tattoo to cover them. He asked his angels to help him find a way out of his life. A few days later he was involved in a terrible car crash while under the influence of drugs. He broke his pelvis very badly. While he was hospitalized and drifting in and out of consciousness, he saw his angel reaching out a hand to him, and he took it. From that day the doctors agreed to help him fight his addiction and his parents took him back because they saw the change in him. He fought his way back one day at a time to a good life. He still has to fight because he knows his addiction is for life, but he also knows for sure that his angels will help him be who he really needs to be. He knows this because his angel told him that the tell-tale scars from the collapsed veins would disappear without the need for a tattoo. When he had his bandages removed from his lacerated arms, the heroin needle marks were gone, replaced by bumpy, but clean, white skin. George thought he wanted money, but bizarrely what he actually *needed* was to be injured in a car crash.

A SENSE OF LOSS

Another example of the wrong energy to have when it comes to having angels hear you is that brought about by grief, though of course it's perfectly understandable to be grief-stricken after suffering a loss. Having lost both my parents and a sister I can fully understand the depths to which grief can drag you. And of course, when a loved one dies, people beg and plead and pray to hear from them again, and can't understand why it usually doesn't happen. They often lose their faith at this point, which only makes things worse. The sad truth is that grief, in all its stages, through disbelief, sorrow, loss, anger and desperation, all come under the heading of 'aggressive negative' energy. It's pretty much normally impossible for anyone to change this energy while they are going through the grieving process, and this is why a loved one is rarely able to come through, because when they do come through, it's always with angelic help, and of course angels can't work in negative energy. I've known people wait ten years to get a sign from someone they've lost, because that's how long it's taken them to get back to a state of positivity. One of the ways to help with this is if you love someone to *tell* them so while you still have them. The most destructive of all emotions after a loss is regret or guilt. So many times people wish they'd said something while the person was alive, but always thought there would be plenty of time for that. The most commonly asked question is, 'Did they know that I loved them?' To avoid this, make sure that the people you love *know* that you love them, so that there will be no doubts.

Sometimes the grief-stricken do believe in angels and the afterlife enough to overcome their sorrow and ask for some help. This next story demonstrates how you can prepare your energy to accept an inevitable loss and, in doing so, you can allow angels to bring a message through – or, if you're really blessed like Elise, actually bring your loved one through.

My father, then in his early eighties, was ageing quickly and was frequently in and out of hospital. I was visiting one weekend when he awoke from sleeping in his armchair with a huge start, looking shocked and afraid.

'Who was that man?' he asked us sharply (several family members were in the living room at the time).

'There was no one there, Dad,' I said to him.

'A man, dressed all in black. He was stood there,' he replied, pointing to the floor in front of him.

He was obviously very shaken and disturbed, and perhaps on some inner level he had an idea who the man in black really was. I had no doubts that this was no dream, so I kept silent. My father had been ill for some time, but as a stubborn, articulate man, whose brain remained totally intact until the day he passed, he refused to give in to something he feared with every fibre of his being. I knew then that he might not last another year, and accepted silently the fact that he would move on to the next part of his journey in the not-too-distant future. In my own spiritual journeying I had come to have an understanding of 'the man in black' visiting the old ones or the sick, or even those whose death may be imminent from some other cause. The 'Angel of Death' appears in many forms, this being one of them. It brings a warning, or sometimes even an invitation, that the time is coming to move on.

When Dad had forgotten the incident a couple of weeks later, we were chatting about this, that and the other in an amiable kind of way.

'Will you make me a promise, Dad?' I asked him.

'Well, if I knew what it was, then maybe,' he replied.

'Will you promise me that, after you die, you'll come back and prove to me that I'm right, that actually there is no death?'

He laughed, but he made me that promise! My father, although Jewish and a founding member of our local synagogue, had no belief in God although he was a Humanist, a true humanitarian and caring man who practised his belief in his love of humanity in the many and varied charitable works that he did until shortly before he passed over. He was terrified of dying, and his fear of the unknown prompted his refusal to give in to the many signposts leading him to the next stage of his journey.

In May the following year my mother, older sister and her husband took their last holiday with my father to one of their favourite destinations in Spain. On their return it seemed painfully obvious that Dad was nearing the end. He became very ill, being admitted to hospital, where he remained after one brief visit home until he was deemed well enough to be transferred to a Jewish nursing home in Clapham. Nightingale's was a home he had specifically chosen himself even though it was at least an hour's drive for any of the family, so none of them would be able to get there in a hurry. The dreaded call came early on 17 August 2007. I'd just completed an assessment for a new client at the doctor's surgery where I worked as a counsellor, and so I didn't get the message on my mobile until after 11 a.m. My younger sister had texted me to ask me to call immediately I received the text. It was time, and a family friend was driving my mother and older sister to the nursing home – they would collect me on the way. I packed my things and drove home as fast as I was able to, and waited for our dear friend to arrive, which he did about ten minutes later.

I often wonder if my father chose the place where he would pass deliberately knowing that it might not be possible for any family member to be able to get there in time to be with him when he moved on. He was a proud man; perhaps he preferred that we remember him the way he used to be: a strong, handsome and capable husband, father and friend to so many. On our arrival, we were greeted by the manager and quietly told that we would be unable to see my father just at that moment. He led us into an office where he informed us that Dad had died peacefully a short while before our arrival.

'Was anyone with him when he died?' I asked.

'Yes … a nurse,' he answered vaguely, which told me that no one had been with my dad at the time of his passing. Something outside of my control then seemed to take me over as we entered my father's room.

I hadn't been fully trained in healing practice but I was in the middle of completing my Master's in Psychotherapy and Healing, and also I'd experienced many forms of spiritual healing myself as a client. It was as if I went into automatic pilot while my mother and sisters sat crying in the bedroom. I stood at the foot of the bed, arms outstretched, quietly asking for divine guidance to assist in the release of my dad's spirit and help him to pass over and move on into the light. I have no idea how long I stood there, and then at some point I moved on and around the body, working with some unseen energy field, eventually moving toward his head. At that point I moved closer and 'worked' with my hands around the top of his body. Eventually it was as though some unseen voice said, 'It is enough, it is done,' and I moved away and held my mother and my sisters to comfort them.

The funeral took place a few days later (in the Jewish faith the funeral is as close to the time of death as possible) and there, again, I instinctively moved toward the coffin, saying whatever prayers came to me and moving my hands around the coffin, asking for further divine guidance should any of his energy or spirit still remain and need assistance moving on. I offered a eulogy afterwards, despite the Rabbi warning me that I might not be able to speak and might break down, but I did not. I adored my father. He was like an unreachable God to me (very Freudian, very Electra!) and in reality we were never as close as I would have wished; nevertheless I loved him with a passion.

Later in the week I went to visit a friend's esoteric shop in Teddington, called 'As It Is', wanting to find something to give my younger sister for her birthday, which fell exactly one week after Dad had died, on 24 August. I wandered round the shop and found a beautiful photograph frame, carved with the forms of angels, and felt I had to buy it and put in a photograph of my father. The energy in the shop is amazing. It's very calm and peaceful; a warm energy that makes you feel like you could stay there for a long, long time. On this particular day it was stronger than ever and I struggled with tears (as I am while writing this!). As I looked at different things, something pulled me across the shop to a shelf where there stood various carvings, statuettes, boxes and so forth. I nearly jumped backwards as a statue virtually jumped off the shelf and fell into my hands. It was a pair of white alabaster hands clasped and holding a tiny baby, and I heard the words, 'I am with God now. I am safe.' As I paid for it along with the frame, the lovely woman in the shop said that she also felt that there was an undoubtedly stronger than usual energy there that day and, interestingly, at that particular time the usually busy shop was empty except for me and the woman at the counter.

That night I had a dream. I was standing in my kitchen with the back door open and my father walked in through the door holding three trays of food. They were large trays, one laden with flat bread, one with meat and one with fish. It was a huge amount of food for two people, and far too much meat for my father, who had had diabetes and high cholesterol, and had suffered heart problems.

I questioned him, asking, 'Dad, how can you eat like this? But I suppose now you're in spirit you're able to eat whatever you like?' and I placed the trays of food in the oven. We sat down at the table looking at each other without any words being spoken as we communicated by thought and energy, and I asked him, 'Dad, how are we able to talk like this now, as we never could while you were alive?' and he answered, 'Because you saved my life.'

In meditation a few days later, I felt the presence of an energy and began to sense the appearance of something in my room. I heard the words, 'I am your father,' and initially thought *Oh, wow, I must be having a serious religious experience here,* until I began to see the faint outline of a man. It was a man who strongly resembled my own father as he had been in his forties. He was very handsome, dark and with a moustache. He came toward me.

'Well,' he said, 'have you heard me yet? I kept my promise!'

'Oh yes, Dad, I've heard you loud and clear – every time. Thank you – but I don't want you to become too tired. If you must move on now then so be it – I love you, Dad. I will always love you.'

At that, I believe he did move on and, although I long to speak with him again (and maybe one day will), that was the last time I really 'heard' him, and it is in the writing of this story that I offer my thanks and sincere gratitude to all of those in body and in spirit without whose help and support this might never have been written.

Blessed be.

I had several experiences during the death of my dad, and following the death of my mum and sister, which are chronicled in other books. Suffice it to say that I received visitations and saw visions for which I have no proof, even to myself, but I have faith that they were real and thank my angels for bringing them to me.

HOW NOT TO ABSORB OTHER PEOPLE'S BAD ENERGY

Of course, even when you've managed to stabilize your own energy, that isn't necessarily the happy ending to the story. Energy 'travels'. It travels between people and pets, and between people and people. Imagine the scene: this morning you dutifully used your Focus Picture before you got out of bed. A Focus Picture is a focus for positive thoughts, which you create by drawing a picture that symbolizes how you would like your life to be, and writing an eight-word mantra around the image. You should take a lot of care over the picture even if you're not a natural artist, because the more effort you make, the more you'll make it 'yours' and the greater its effect will be. The words can be anything that comes to mind, and you'll be surprised to find that wherever you start reading the circle of words, and whichever direction you read them in, they will form into an intelligible chain of thought. By staring at this image every morning before you even get out of bed, and repeating the mantra several times, you'll set your day up to go positively and lessen the impact of any negative events. So, there you are buzzing with positive energy, walking down the road, humming a little tune, heading to somewhere you're looking forward to. You feel close to your angels, things are going well, and then it happens. You bump into Ms Grumpy. She stops you and starts to tell you all her troubles. For a while the Focus Picture works. (And the more you use it, the more it will work.) Your energy stays positive and you still feel good.

But you haven't been doing this for very long, and she's a past master at dumping on people, and that means energy as well as words. Gradually she starts to wear you down. Maybe you start to feel sorry for her, and you think, *well, I have to feel sorry for this poor woman – look at all the bad stuff she's had to go through.* Unfortunately, 15 minutes later Ms Grumpy goes off with a smile on her face, having unloaded all her negative energy onto you, and your day and your good energy level are potentially ruined.

What could you have done differently?

This part is all about your *aura* – that energy field that surrounds all living things, and surrounds you, too. You have to learn to build defences around it. Eventually you'll just defend your energy naturally, but for now you need to do it consciously. When you spot Ms Grumpy coming, you don't have to avoid her if you don't want to, although, deliberately or not, she is harming your energy when she dumps on you, so you wouldn't be a bad person if you sidestepped her once in a while. What you do is quickly visualize your aura as a big white bubble of light all around you. Fill it with sparkles if it helps you visualize it. And here comes Ms Grumpy. Her aura, if you could see it, is all muddy and dark – not what your sparkles need to make them shine! Poor Ms Grumpy is what I call a *psychic vampire*.

There are two more things you can do: quickly visualize your chakras, those spinning wheels that emit your energy and also absorb energy – all seven of them in a line down your body, as flowers. Make sure each one is tightly closed up into a bud. Then, secondly, visualize the front of your aura transforming itself into a mirror. Push this mirror in a bowed shape out toward the oncoming person. You can do all of this in seconds if you practise it.

When Ms Grumpy reaches you, several things will happen. She won't be able to stand as close to you as she would have liked, and in the way that she usually does, which has always made you feel uncomfortable. She'll be stopped by the 'bow wave' of your aura, and just like the bow wave of a ship pushes water aside, you'll force her aura, and therefore her physical body, back. She won't be able to 'invade your space'. Instead, you'll have made your space bigger. Then, when she starts her diatribe, you can just stand there and have some sympathy for the woman, but her energy won't be able to get through to your chakras. They'll be safe, tightly budded and behind that mirror, which will bounce the negative energy back at her. She'll also move on quicker than she usually does, because she won't get that satisfied feeling she usually gets from draining herself onto you. Of course, you should help her if you can, in a practical way; just don't get energetically entangled and let her muddy your waters.

The same thing happens sometimes with people who habitually phone you up to dump bad news on you; you can virtually feel their negative vibes humming down the phone line at you. After a call from them you always feel empty and lacking in life-force. The barrier this time should obviously be pushed toward the phone, and it will have the same effect on the caller as it did on Ms Grumpy.

Of course sympathy is something that we as humans should feel, and we shouldn't feel bad about that, but it isn't an assertive positive emotional state, and it can actually damage your ability to help others. This is not because it's negative, but because it makes your own energy weaker, and this means you can't boost someone with your own positive energy, which is often the best, and sometimes the only way you can help them – this is also true when dealing with distressed animals. Your weak energy, if you feel too sorry for them, can actually weaken them too and prevent their rehabilitation.

You can take the same protective measures that you used with Ms Grumpy if you're in your car and can sense danger of accident or the sparks of road rage growing all around you. This time, push the bubble out all the way round you, like an expanding balloon, encompassing the whole car in its protective field. This takes a bit more practice, but it can be done – as can be seen from mine and my husband's miraculous escape from serious injury described earlier (page xix). In the case of incipient road rage, you'll find that putting up your barrier means that other drivers ignore you and don't seem to feel a need to vent their anger on you and/or your car.

Another example of negative energy attacking yours is when you bump into one of those friends who seem to argue against everything you say. Or they tell you their problems over and over, seemingly begging for some advice, but when you offer a suggestion they always have an 'Ah but' to throw your help back at you. As well as using the methods above, one way to try and help this kind of friend is to ask them, bluntly, 'What good things have you got in your life?' Any little thing you can get them to say, and therefore focus on, will help their energy start to lean toward the positive instead of the negative. But always remember in all cases that your ultimate number one loyalty should be to your own soul and its progress. Don't be afraid to say, 'No,' because a good, true friend will still like you even if you can't help them on this occasion! On the other hand, if they're just using you and become affronted when you have to say 'No' sometimes, then you don't really need them in your life at all.

This is especially true if they continually make you angry because of their attitude to life in general. Anger is one of the most destructive emotional states out there, so you don't need it!

The more you can live your life using your instinct and intuition, the quicker you'll be able to be like an animal (or an angel) and see people as *energy* rather than as just their names. That way you can also learn to *deal* with them as energy, and know just what to do to keep yourself and your own energy running smoothly. The more you train yourself to do this, the better at it you'll become and the easier it will be for your angels to lock into you.

OFFLOADING THE NEGATIVE ENERGY

Until you learn to deal with your life efficiently, handling energy like second nature, it's a good idea to empty out all the negative stuff in the evening, out in the garden, as soon as you get home. Visualize a tap low down on your abdomen and open it, seeing all the inky negative energy you've picked up during the day flowing away into the earth. It's better to work outdoors for this because then you have nothing between you and the planet, whereas indoors you have material in between, and you could end up inadvertently channelling it into your home, which is of course the last thing you want! You won't do any harm to the planet this way, because Mother Nature and the universe have ways of safely using the dark energy you give it. Look upon it as the ultimate in recycling! The negative energy you expel is turned into 'dark matter', or 'dark flow' as physicists are starting to call it. I like to call this stuff God's plasticine, because he really can mould it into whatever he wants.

Another way to help keep your chakras clear of negative influences is always, always to wear crystals. With the current fashion for 'bling' it's very easy to make yourself trendy *and* safe with the appropriate jewellery. If in doubt as to which to use, you can play safe with quartz and amethyst.

The next chapter contains some wonderful stories that readers have sent to me. Some of them bring up yet another angel conundrum: you'll notice that in some of them the people are displaying classic 'negative' energy traits, mostly fear. So how come they got their prayers answered? Surely only positive energy enables help to arrive? That obviously isn't the case, as there are thousands of stories that feature spiritual intervention coming into a negative situation. There's an important difference between these cases, though, and the cases of people who have been desperately trying for years to get help, starting from times of trouble and despair and continuing that way. As I described earlier, a negative energy state is like turbulent air around a tiny plane and the angels are the refuelling plane that can't get connected because of the bumpy ride. Or I sometimes talk about negative energy as a boat adrift on an ocean, the waves created by the negative energy preventing an angel, represented by another boat or raft, coming close.

Here is the good – in fact, excellent – news. Once you make a strong connection to your angels, you're 'tethered' to them. Imagine that tiny boat or plane, and then imagine that there's a strong lifeline stretching between it and the angel boat or plane, firmly attached at both ends. Despite rough weather, with the right attitude you can still haul them together. It's like pushing a plug into an electric socket. Afterwards you can twist and shake the wire (with negative energy) but the connection is still live. So long as, in that time of need, you can *smooth your energy enough* not to strain the lifeline or the cable too much, despite your fear, or anger, etc., then the current can still flow and the help can still arrive. This means, of course, that once you establish a link with your angels at some point in your life, from then on you'll get help in any situation, so long as the angels know that it's right for your spiritual progress for you to do so.

MOST IMPORTANT FACT

Don't be afraid! Any time you feel a spark of fear
coursing through your mind, igniting a flame as it
goes, cover it and capture it, and then let your angel's
wings smother it.

CHAPTER 3

Stories of Angels Who Have Heard Our Prayers and Answered Them

Naturally I get sent hundreds of letters from people who have asked their angels for help and received it, and also from people who didn't exactly ask for help but got it anyway because they had the right energy. I'd like to share some of them with you here.

An uncle, whom I thought the world of, passed really unexpectedly and suddenly, which left us all in shock. A difficult situation meant I couldn't attend his funeral and not being able to say goodbye made me feel so sad, but I knew I could do it in my own way. On the day of the funeral I put up a photo of my uncle in the lounge next to the stereo and I said, 'I'm going to play you an Elvis song, as I know how much you like his music.' I got the CD out of the cupboard and sat on the floor, took the disc out of the case and placed the case on the floor while I put the disc into the stereo. As I reached down to pick up the case to choose a song to play, I saw that a beautiful white feather lay on top of it. It wasn't there before. I instantly burst into tears and felt a huge surge of comfort envelop me. I truly feel an angel helped me that day.

– *Gail*

I agree with Gail that an angel helped her that day. The angel sensed that Gail was distressed and grieving (negative states) but also that she was accepting the situation and also was expectant that she would be helped to say goodbye in her own way. So, because Gail was already connected, already tethered to her angels, her relatively balanced energy enabled her to be helped.

On the day that I did my *shanka prakshalana* (yogic cleansing) I definitely felt a presence as I had prayed/asked my angels and guides to be with me that day, and I had dedicated that day to ridding my life of alcohol. That was three and a half years ago and, thanks to their help, I haven't wanted or drunk alcohol since. Also, on advice from one of your books, I asked my angels to communicate on my behalf with my son Kim's angels to help him find his way. My son would abuse me via e-mail and telephone, and our relationship was disastrous. Prior to that I'd been asking my angels to help him direct, but there hadn't been any real change as a result. After reading *Angel Whispers* I asked my angels to talk to Kim's angels instead, and to help him to find his way, amongst other things, and lo and behold, what a change! He has become a new person! Kim was in Denmark at the time, during August and September. He was doing a show and staying with his father. When he returned home to Australia, to stay once again at our place, there was a real change in him. He apologized for how he'd been treating me, and not once did he abuse me right up until he left for Queensland at the end of October.

Since then, his phone calls to me have been just to say hello (not asking for money or complaining) and to tell me that he is well and happy. The fact that I can have a decent conversation with him now is just amazing.

– Linda

This story illustrates that you can't ask your angels to interfere in someone else's life. The only way you can get help to another person is to ask your angels to talk to that person's angels. Then if those angels feel it to be the right thing, and the right time, they will help. I really feel that Linda and her son may have past-life issues, which have been coming between them. It seems that Kim's angels have at least partially healed those past-life issues, hence the change in Kim's attitude to his mum. If he were to go for past-life therapy, it might improve matters between him and his mother even more. And if Linda were to go, she might finally understand why he treated her as he did, and with that understanding would come a lessening of pain.

I had an angel experience when I asked for love. I saw pink in my mind and I felt a presence around me. Then I felt my fringe being moved and felt my forehead being touched. Also, while doing angel card readings a few years ago, I kept getting the healing card, and soon a flyer came through my door about Reiki healing. I started doing Reiki, and then years later, on another occasion when learning to communicate better with angels, I saw in my mind a crystal ball being placed in my hand and I could feel the palm of my hand with something in it. I felt my hand being closed over it and then I got told, 'The gift is in your hand.'

– *Caroline*

Caroline not only got the love she asked for, but her angel expanded on that connection to show her part of her path in this life. I'm sure as time goes by, she'll get more guidance.

I was stranded on the side of a road in a rural area with no one in sight and my husband had gone walking for help (this was before cellphones). After he'd gone it felt very lonely out there on the highway, and I started viewing every occasional passing car with suspicion. I locked myself inside the car. Sure enough, a very scary man stopped his car and offered to drive me for help. I declined and stayed locked in the car, praying that he would go away, and eventually he did. I got out of the car to look up the road to see if my husband was coming back, all the while praying to God for help, but there was no sign of my husband. Then suddenly, I turned around and there was a man in a white jeep pulling up. I hadn't even seen the vehicle approaching, but for some unfathomable reason I didn't feel at all uneasy. The man seemed to know exactly what we needed and he had water in his jeep to put in the radiator. I told him that it was amazing that he was there with water and all, and he said something I thought was a little odd. He said, 'That is just something we do.' The word 'we' made me wonder. And if he was just a man out helping people with car trouble, why was he dressed all in white? That didn't seem logical. His jeep wasn't like the Jeep Cherokee style SUV types; it was the old open-top military style jeep (except that it was all white, which in itself was odd!). It reminded me of the promise of an army of angels to protect us.

– Kathleen

Kathleen's powerful story demonstrates beautifully one of those times when a guardian will step in regardless, to prevent something going wrong. Even though at the time of connection Kathleen was in a negative state of energy (fear), because this was an event that wasn't meant to go the way it did, her guardian was still able to help her. Of course Kathleen was one of those people who'd already connected to her angels previously.

Janet Russell is a TV producer in New York and I've had the pleasure of being a guest on her show. She's also a well-known medium. She recently told me this story about her daughter, which once again shows the connection between children and their angels.

I know that angels are real, because there was a time when my daughter was very ill in the hospital with MRSA and spinal meningitis, and all of a sudden she said that

It may seem that a lost lilo is a pretty trivial thing for an angel to help out with. In fact I even had someone criticize me for telling people to ask their angels for trivial things, like lost handbags, saying that angel energy surely shouldn't be wasted on something so meaningless. But in cases like this, it isn't so much the act, but the sign. Julie was in the right frame of energy at the time, and her angel saw a good opportunity to prove its existence to her. She was then able to be open enough to go ahead and meet Henry. Without that apparently trivial incident, she might not have been able to do it. I will continue to tell people to start asking their angel for help with small requests, and a lost lilo comes perfectly under that heading.

When I was 18 years old and very impressionable, I fell in love with a boy called Kevin. Of course I thought the sun rose in his eyes, but after a while he betrayed me and dumped me. I was so upset I thought I'd die. As far as I was concerned, love was over for me. I thought I'd never find anyone else to love me. But I used every ounce of my strength, told my angels that I trusted them and tried to throw myself into my life. Just a couple of days later I was standing outside a shop in the mall when someone touched my shoulder very lightly. I turned around to see a strange-looking young man, dressed quite raggedly and looking pretty dirty. My impulse was to pull back, but something in his eyes made me stay close to him. He said, 'Stop worrying so much, dear heart.' (A strange and old-fashioned thing to call me!) 'Your life will come back on track and one day you'll even have a son. You'll call him Arthur.' I had to smile because I couldn't ever imagine calling a son by such a dated name. The young man turned and walked away, and he moved very strangely, too, almost like his feet were a couple of inches off the ground.

Just two years later I met Gary and it was love at first sight. We had a son two years after that and I did call him Arthur, not really because I'd come to love it or because of what I'd been told, but because Gary's dad, granddad and great-granddad were all called Arthur.

– Jacky

Jacky's acceptance and her positive energy in the face of what to her at the time was a tragedy enabled her angel not only to help her but to sow the seed of future proof of its existence. It was no coincidence that she went on to have a child and find that it 'just turned out' to be appropriate to call him by that name.

Last summer my partner, Andrew, bought me a pack of angel cards. I loved them and started reading everything that I could find about angels. Very shortly thereafter I started feeling very peaceful about myself and started meditating, and asked the angels for a sign that they did indeed exist. Three days later Andrew and I visited a very old church and decided to take some photos. Andrew wanted one of me, so I walked about 30 feet away so he could take it. As I stood there I heard a laugh and turned to see a lovely old man sitting on a bench to my right, smiling at me, and he said, 'Ha ha! I am going to be in your photo now!' I laughingly said back, 'Well, I don't mind at all.' We downloaded the photos on getting home and there was nobody sitting on the bench. I believe the old man was an angel sent to reassure me that angels were indeed real, and to tell me that I was on the right path.

– Janette

I've always known that angels have a sense of humour, and Janette's certainly did!

Simon's angel had his work cut out to prove his existence, but he was certainly there when he was needed.

I'm a long-distance HGV driver for a small company, and I started there quite young. I was about 22 years old. My parents were always worried about me and always insisted that I called them whenever I got to my destination so that they'd know I was all right. They hated all the miles I did on motorways in particular, as these roads are notoriously dangerous. However, when danger did come it was on a country road. My Nanna used to smile when Mum and Dad voiced their worries, and say, 'He'll be all right; can't you see that light of angels around him?' Since when, though, do people listen to their parents? Mum and Dad still worried. Nanna would chat to me and encourage me in 'nonsense' as my parents called it. But I loved her stories of angels helping people, and I liked to think I did have an angel.

This night I was heading toward home and the truck was empty, which was a good thing! It was a dark country road with no street lighting, a few miles from the M6, which I was heading for. I don't like driving lanes at night in my car because the glare of approaching lights can be awful, but in the truck I was higher and it wasn't so much of a problem. Due to that I was able to see what the driver coming the other way couldn't. There was a stag standing in the road. It was a big red deer, and I knew that when the driver of the oncoming car saw it, he'd swerve, because if he hit it, it would destroy his car. It might seem stupid that he'd come at me in my several ton truck instead, but that's human nature for you.

We tend to react to the immediate. Sure enough the car swerved onto my side of the road. I was already breaking in anticipation, but it wasn't going to stop the inevitable collision. I had to turn the wheel left toward the hedges, because at least I'd give the car driver and maybe passengers, if he had any, some help to survive. The truck wheels went into a ditch I hadn't seen, though, and it was my vehicle that went off the road and tumbling into a field. The car apparently missed the truck by inches. As I realized that the field was actually a hill, and that my truck was going to somersault down it, I was scared for a moment, but then I heard Nanna's words in my head, and for the first time I actually saw and felt the white light around me. It was like I was in a bubble. The noise of the truck as it hurtled toward its doom, as inevitable as a dying dinosaur, was horrendous, but I wasn't afraid. I felt my body being catapulted around the cab, but I didn't feel any pain. When the noise and the motion finally stopped, all I could hear was the hissing of hot water from the radiator and, outside, only silence. There had been four people in the car and they all came running, not a scratch on them, expecting, judging by their voices, to find a dead body smashed to pieces. They dragged open the driver's door and stopped dead, as if they'd seen a ghost, when I looked calmly at them.

When I looked at my trashed truck from outside afterwards, I could see why they were so amazed to find me not only not dead, but unhurt. There was no way I should have walked away from that crash. After that day my parents didn't laugh at Nanna any more.

MOST IMPORTANT FACT

It's well worth all the effort of connecting with your angels initially, despite the time and application it takes, because once you're 'plugged in', you'll have the connection for life and when you need help you won't always have to ask, because they'll be there on hand and ready to step in.

CHAPTER 4

How Close to the Angels Can We Get?

If your energy is positive and calm enough, and you manage to connect with angels, you can get very close indeed. There are many levels of connection, just as there are many levels of angels. The four kinds that I feel are the most accessible and the most relevant to life as a human are what I call: odd job angels, guardian angels, master path angels and soul angels.

Let's take a closer look at each of these.

ODD JOB ANGELS

These are more little bursts of electrical energy than actual entities. They often appear as little black dots, sometimes as big as a small mouse or large spider that you see out of the corner of your eye. They can often be glimpsed in the evening, especially if you have a light-coloured carpet so that they show up better. Normally in this case they vanish as soon as you look right at them. You can become quite cunning, though, and watch them for quite a while if you just use the corner of your eye and don't focus on them. They can, though, also be manifested by your own electrical energy into something that can be seen a lot more easily.

For instance, on the day that Tony discovered he'd passed his exam to become a Driving Instructor, several years ago, he was very elated at having succeeded. As he sat relaxing and basking in the feeling of achievement, he could see a whole swarm of tiny coloured lights, like mini Christmas tree lights, whizzing around his head, in much the same way as a crowd of flies might circle a lampshade. He was able to sit and watch them for some time before they vanished.

Another time I saw a whole column of them, coalescing into a column of light violet in the corner of the bedroom. There was no particular reason for them that time. I had just emerged from a very deep meditation, which might have been what attracted them.

I don't think you could ever touch these little beings as such, but if you're lucky enough to see them as lights the way we have, you can walk or move into them. If you do you'll get a sensation like tiny pins and needles, a gentle buzz, not unpleasant. Afterwards you'll feel energized as if you'd just stood under a pounding shower.

GUARDIAN ANGELS

These beings can get very close to their charges. They can appear in any form they choose, and when they manifest into a physical being, like a man, woman, child or even animal, they can touch and be touched, just like a human can. They can appear as a butterfly or dragonfly commonly, and in those cases they can alight on the person they're watching over or bring through a passed-over loved one for.

If they come to intervene to save a person from an accident, they can actually become very tactile, and many a person has felt a shove from their guardian, which has pushed them out of danger. Take Maggie, who sent me this:

Way back in the early 1980s I was working late nights in a milk bar in Perth, Australia ... No ordinary milk bar, mind you. We offered wonderful ice-cream concoctions by the names of Merry Widow, Paluca, Sunset Dreams and heaps more. The American Navy had just started its stops in Perth for 'R & R', so this Saturday evening we were really busy and did not get away until after 1 a.m.

Now, usually I would have gotten a cab home, but with all those sailors lined up and waiting for cabs I decided it would be quicker to walk home. Hey, it was only around 40 minutes and the night was warm and gorgeous.

But it soon became apparent that I was being followed. I crossed the street and so did he. I ran. He ran. He was so close at all times, roughly 10 to 15 feet away. I could see him clearly at all times. This must have given him a real buzz.

About halfway home I got to the causeway, a bridge that spans the Swan River. Ahead of me was a huge dark park area, and by this time I was in real panic mode. I remember shouting, 'Hey God! Anytime now, help!'

A cab drew up next to me, the other side of the metal railings. It was driving into oncoming traffic and the driver didn't seem aware that anything was unusual, and that the passenger door was on the wrong side.

The driver reached across, opened the door, and said, 'Margaret, get in.' Now, whenever I was in deep poo I was called Margaret, so naturally I did as I was asked. Somehow I walked through the metal railings. They simply ceased to be there. I've tried this many times since, and only received the gift of bruises. I was driven directly home without the driver ever asking for the address. On reaching the house the driver asked for my house keys, opened the door and let me in.

Then he handed the keys back and said, 'We will meet again.' He never charged me for the cab or anything. I remember that the cab was shiny black and smelled of new leather and honey. The driver was shiny clean – that's the only way I can describe it – and wearing a really, really white shirt.

Now, me being me and caught up in the day-to-day stuff of work and rearing three children, I let this miracle pass until around three weeks later when a newspaper article described how a girl had been found in the park by the causeway, raped, beaten and left for dead. I was really feeling sick and the indenti-photo only confirmed the feeling. It was the same man who had followed me. I will never know how close I came to a dreadful experience, or why I was saved, but I'll always thank the angel who came to my rescue. I now know that angel to be Gabriel, for we have indeed met many times since, and he continues to guide and protect me.

Wasn't it interesting that Maggie's angel knew to call her by the name Margaret, just to make sure she obeyed?

Our guardian angels can move or manipulate other physical objects in order to get a message through, as with Sophia, who told me this amazing story of her journey to a particular enlightenment:

The little boy was totally immersed in his game. He crawled about, moving his small plastic figures around, in the dust of the front garden of a terraced house as I passed by, and I wouldn't have even noticed him except for his cry of 'Skywalker! You will die!' There it was again, a reference to the word 'sky'. What on Earth was going on? It had started when I woke up in the morning to my radio alarm playing the song 'Sky' by Sonique. I noticed because it was an unusual sort of choice for my local radio station, but I'd thought no more about it. I went down to the tube and that's when I started to get a weird feeling that something was going on. Nearly all the hoardings had the word 'sky' in them. Ocean Sky Jets, Sky Insurance, Sky Bingo. It was crazy. I walked along starting to wonder if I should take some notice of all these insane coincidences. I started to think I was some sort of Chicken Little and the sky was going to fall on me! Then I came to a poster that didn't mention the word, and I sighed with relief, for a moment anyway. Then I saw that the poster had a corner that wasn't stuck down properly, revealing several layers of old posters underneath. My curiosity got the better of me and I pulled the corners back. Sure enough, a couple of layers down, there was an old advert for the film *Vanilla Sky*. I was getting a little freaked out by then. My train came and I got on. I didn't know what else to do. It started again. The ads on the tube train all had the same theme. The posters right opposite me were for Stars in the Sky Dating Agency and SkyTours. My head started to buzz and I felt fuzzy and faint. Something was going on. I was getting some sort of warning or message, but what was the point if I couldn't understand them? I scanned my fellow passengers. I think everyone who travels on the tube does that nowadays. I don't know exactly what we think we're going to see. A man in a hoodie with the word 'bomb' on his rucksack or something! Everyone looked normal – well, as normal as a random selection of commuters all crammed unnaturally together like sardines, trying not to invade each other's personal space as much as possible, could look. But anyway, I thought, what would the word 'sky' have to do with a terrorist on a tube train? I got to my station without incident, rode up the escalator, numbly passing an ad for Sky TV, and then walked through some residential streets toward the office where I worked. That was when I heard the boy playing in his tiny front garden. I really didn't know what

I was supposed to do about all this. So I walked on, puzzling over it. As I waited to cross the street, standing on a narrow pavement, I glanced across the road, almost already knowing what I'd see. There was a huge hoarding advertising a film called *Look to the Sky*. Suddenly something clicked in my brain, and without thinking anymore I turned and sprinted from my place on the curb as quickly as I could. Instantly there was a terrifyingly loud crashing sound, and sharp particles snapped into me, peppering the back of my neck with tiny nicks. I stopped and for a moment I was frozen to the spot, unable to turn around, feeling my head for injuries, but finding only red dust particles. Eventually, as silence fell, I turned round. There on the pavement where I'd been standing, and scattered all over the road I'd been about to cross, were the remains of a large Victorian chimney pot. I looked up and saw, three storeys above me, the snapped off remains of the stack. Apart from the tiny nicks, I was untouched. If I hadn't moved fast the pot would have hit me on the head, and I'm pretty sure I would have been lying there dead right then. More red dust floated in front of me on the air and I stared at the swirling shapes incredulously as the cloud seemed to form the shape of two outstretched wings.

Is it possible that my guardian angel knew exactly where I'd be standing and at exactly what time? Did my angel know that the chimney pot, which must have been loose and tottering in the wind for days, was going to fall on that spot at exactly the time I was going to be standing there? Were there an usual amount of repetitions of the word 'sky' around that day, put there by my angel, or had my subconscious been programmed while I slept to be especially receptive to that word so that I'd get the message? I don't honestly know, but I do know that I missed death by inches that day, and it was because of the 'message' that I avoided it.

This story comes from Emma, who has always gone to great lengths to get as close as possible to her angels:

My first experience began with Archangel Raphael. At the time I needed healing from stress relating to college and family life in general, and I had no one to turn to. As a kid I had always had a huge belief in angels and other realms, and the belief carried on all through to adulthood. Around four to five years ago was when the experiences started, and at that time I was 16 years of age. I hadn't been meditating for that long so I thought *why not?* and *give it a go and see what happens*. Honestly, I wasn't really expecting anything to happen, but how wrong I was.

I closed my eyes and simply called out to Archangel Raphael, and started explaining my situation, and about two minutes after I asked, I felt some fingers gently brush against my forehead. It kind of felt like a cool breeze; this caught my attention and I immediately opened my eyes. No windows were open and nothing was there physically that could have caused the breeze. To this day I still believe it was Raphael showing me in his own way that he had heard my request for help.

As time went on, Raphael was the only Archangel I talked to for at least a month or two, and he told me many wonderful things. He told me about being an incarnated angel, and gave information and images about my past life as a nurse in Bulgaria in the 1700s. I used to let my ego get the better of me and let it make me believe it was all my imagination. I went through a phase where I thought I had totally lost my mind, but I soon got over this when I had it all confirmed by another angel reader, and I knew this wasn't my imagination and it was all real.

When I was about 17 years old, I wanted to continue what I was doing and was excited to meet the other Archangels. The second angel to come to me was Archangel Michael, and Michael is the angel that has helped me the most. He has become a very dear friend to me. I used to look at pictures of Archangel Michael on Google, and many images showed him with a sword. This sometimes made me feel reluctant to talk to him and I wondered what his personality was like. Was he like Raphael? But when I first talked to Michael I found him to be very sweet and he has a very strong fatherly quality to him, but he can also be amusing and never fails to make you laugh and cheer you up.

As I said, Michael has helped me with so much, especially with cutting cords from other people, situations and feelings that haven't been serving my highest good and have been pulling me down. Michael has told me many times that he 'has my back', which he always says with a grin on his face.

From the ages of 17 to 19 I only felt the angels' energy; I had not yet begun to see them, well not until I reached 20 years old. Turning 20, my connection with the Archangels was improving daily and I was having angel experiences every day. It happens so often it's got to a point now where it's normal for me to hear one of the angels say something to me or feel their energy, and I enjoy their company.

At the age of 20 I was still meditating and I started working on my chakras, especially my third eye, as I wanted to see my angels as well as just hearing and feeling them, and it wasn't an easy task for me as I had major issues visualizing and would constantly get frustrated. At these times I would hear Michael slightly laughing at my reaction and telling me to have patience, and that I'd get the hang of it eventually, and since I had no choice I did finally get the hang of visualizing my chakras. At that point I was rather surprised at how fast my third eye opened. I found that chakra to open much more quickly than my other chakras and I did this for a total of four weeks, and then I started to see things and would become very jumpy as it was something I had not yet got used to.

The first thing I saw was a wing fluttering in the corner of my left eye while I was watching television one afternoon. Seeing things started in my peripheral vision, but the wing I saw that day was clear and I saw enough to make out what it was. I saw the movement and colour, but it would still vanish as soon as I looked straight toward it. However, it always returned when I looked away again.

As the weeks went by I saw angel flashes or angel sparkles, whatever you call them yourself, and the first angel flash I saw was Archangel Gabriel. It was a beautiful golden light that suddenly flashed brightly, and then just vanished. Since then I've seen Gabriel do this many times, even outside of my home, in unlikely places like the back seat of my car.

One thing that I didn't take into account was that, because I had opened my psychic sight, I would see other things besides the angels themselves, and that wasn't always pleasant or enjoyable. I would see shadows, or as some people call them, shadow people, and just random spirits walking around. I remember being in my parents' room and turning around and seeing the spirit of an elderly gentleman just staring at me, and then he vanished. Again this is something Archangel Michael helped me with, and made me feel safe and calm about.

Once I was used to seeing and also hearing people and angels talk to me, I wanted to meet my guardian angel and know so much about him or her. I was surprised how quickly my guardian angel responded. I found out his name is Trevor, and he's very beautiful. I always see him with blond hair, which is shoulder length and which he has in plaits at one side of his face. He has blue eyes, and sometimes appears wearing casual clothes, such as a jeans and a white t-shirt. He also had a love heart tattoo on his right shoulder. Even though he's not as talkative as Michael, Raphael and the other Archangels, I know he's still there when I need him.

By the end of 2009 I would see the angels normally and no longer in my peripheral vision. I would see them walking around and interacting with me as a physical person would be doing. I no longer have to meditate to see them and it's something I enjoy, and they continue to show themselves to me that way. I used to ask Michael many times why it didn't happen sooner, but Michael would respond that I hadn't been ready yet and that I had to get over the fear.

Many people ask me what the angels look like, and really this is a question I can't answer 100 per cent because I always explain that the angels will appear to you in a way you will feel comfortable with, and will show themselves to each individual differently. But to me personally, all the Archangels are very tall, much taller than an average human man. Michael and Raphael appear to me at least seven to eight feet tall. They don't always show their wings, but they can change their appearance whenever they like.

MASTER PATH ANGELS

Some people call these Archangels, but I prefer the term Master Path, because that's what they do – try and steer us onto the right pathway for us by any means possible. These are the angels that can bring dramatic breakthroughs and make our dreams come true. They can change lives in a second and are often responsible, for instance, for the millionaire who suddenly gives most of her money to charity, or the drug dealer who suddenly turns his life around and tries to make up for his past by helping youngsters get their lives back under control. They can be responsible for getting people to 'come out' about themselves, whether it be a person who is gay and has been hiding it from the world, or the wife-beater who realizes that he has to take anger management classes. Or they can be responsible for the most breathtaking, life-saving divine interventions, when someone is saved just because he was not meant to die, in a situation that should have proved fatal. These are the miracle workers.

CBN News in the USA carried the miracle story of Rick and Theresa Hester and their little girl Elise. She was playing the drums in a music store when an SUV, travelling at over 100mph, crashed into the wall, demolishing it and travelling right over the top of the very drum kit that Elise had been playing, completely destroying it. The vehicle was going so fast that it then passed right through the next wall into the store next door. Theresa had been sitting in front of the drum set, with her daughter behind her when the wall burst in. As the choking dust cleared, Elise's mother could still see only a few feet ahead of her, and the floor was covered in pieces of debris, including that of the drum set. Rick heard Theresa calling for their daughter, but there was no response. How could there be? They had to know that their daughter must have been crushed. At that point all Theresa could think of, she said, was that if her little girl was gone, she couldn't bear to live herself. Suddenly, out of the dust and debris Rick and Theresa saw a small figure emerge. The strangest thing was that the little girl came from way in the back of the store, nowhere near where the drums had been. When, later, her parents asked her how she'd got away from the drums in time, Elise said that Jesus had picked her up and carried her to safety. She said he carried her with one hand, because his hands were so big that she fitted there. She said that Jesus kissed her cheek, and that he was 'bigger than the whole world'. Was this really Jesus, or does it make sense that Elise's angel would appear that way, knowing that the little girl wouldn't be afraid if she had Jesus helping her? Either way, it was a wonderful miracle.

SOUL ANGELS

These angels are with your soul when it transits from life to death. Before we're born we have a master plan, a definite goal in this lifetime. It's something we know we have to do, and it can vary from becoming a world leader to something as simple as unfinished business from a previous life that we have to complete. The problem is that once we're born, parents, peers, partners, teachers and bosses change us. They don't mean to, but they do. Our soul angels are always trying to jog our memories, knock our subconscious into 'go' mode, and they do this by nudging us along with past-life clues. If they succeed in waking us up, our whole lives will take on new meaning. More than this – these angels' own progress depends on, and is tied to, ours. This is something else that makes them different.

When the soul angels succeed in their ultimate goal, that of getting us to realize that we have had many lives, and the purpose behind those many lives, it's a kind of 'passing out' for them, too. The fact that their future development depends on ours makes sense to me, because I believe that all souls and spirits must progress to make their existence have meaning. So by completing their task, which can take up to 85 of our human lifetimes, soul angels are able to move up closer to their creator. This means that we help them in the same way they help us.

MOST IMPORTANT FACT

If you ask an angel for help, don't concern
yourself with the 'how'. Just trust, because
that's how miracles happen.

CHAPTER 5

Helping Our Children Stay Connected to Their Angels

All children have an innate and natural connection to their angels, because all children are born with the right energy. Most are sadly changed as they grow older, and the priorities of our world are forced upon them. They lose touch with the fact that we are meant to enjoy life as much as possible. Gradually they lose touch with their intuition, and their energy changes as the fears of their parents, relatives, teachers and grown-ups in general push them into a state of negative energy. Some of them are fortunate enough to keep the positive energy, and some of them can even manage to teach grown-ups a thing or two about instinctive faith. One such child is the son of Phil, who told me this lovely tale.

My wife is Thai – and a Buddhist. They believe strongly in guardian angels. We visit her homeland annually and last year during our visit to Thailand a strange thing happened. We have separate beds because I am a restless sleeper and twist and turn quite a bit. You know when you wake up in the middle of the night: you wake up, and you keep your eyes shut because you really don't want to wake up but would rather go back to sleep. You may open your eyes – just a little bit – to see what time it is, and then try to get back to sleep.

This particular night, in the early hours of the morning, I woke up – wide awake – with my eyes wide open. I didn't start up, I just lay there, wide awake. At the foot of my wife's bed was a shadow – something like the old Sandman shape, but without the hat. It stood, facing my wife, and was about 5½ feet tall. It was totally in shadow so I saw no distinguishing features. It wasn't sinister, and I did not feel horror, fear or any other sense of foreboding. In fact I felt quite calm and relaxed. I sensed that whatever it was became aware that I had seen it and slowly it drifted to the far side and along the side of my wife's bed, slowly disappearing, downwards, until it had disappeared entirely by the time it got to her head. Just as if it were going down a set of stairs.

I was not dreaming. I was wide awake and lay there for a while waiting for it to reappear. It did not. I said nothing to anyone until several days later when my wife and her son were talking about something that had happened to them. I told them just what I have told you, and they showed no surprise or disbelief.

'Oh,' said her son, 'That was my mum's guardian angel!'

I am now a believer!

It's my belief that babies who die in miscarriages are, in a lot of cases, just completing a dress rehearsal. These little souls know that they're going to have a hard time getting unscathed into the world, and so they come through partially, sometimes once and sometimes several times, until the physical link is strong enough to make it to live birth. No soul is ever lost. I have also seen evidence that these babies have a special angel watching over them, and the description has been similar enough on many occasions to prove to me that it is the same angel, or one of an identical group. The baby's mother has been the person to describe this angel to me in every case.

Karen is another such mother and she shares her story with us.

I met a girl called Jacqui several years ago. We both opened our businesses on the same day about 200 yards from each other. Instantly we became friends. Jacqui owns a health food shop which also has a treatment room. I called in for a cup of herbal tea and Jacqui offered to do an angel card reading. I had never heard of angel cards and Jacqui explained it all. We talked for hours about it and I was very interested. I knew that I had strong feelings on the subject and couldn't explain why. I found it very absorbing.

Within four weeks of opening our new businesses we both found out on the same day that we were pregnant! How amazing! Neither of us could believe how much our lives were similar. Sadly I had a miscarriage. But I am a strong person and just got on with things. After a few weeks Jacqui mentioned her 'angel friend' who did crystal work and worked with the angels to help people. I really wanted to go along. I needed to feel different. I booked an appointment with Paula Angel (a nickname I gave her!).

It was a transformational day. When I arrived we had a chat. She asked was there any reason why I had come or what I wanted to achieve. Of course, I broke down in tears. I was devastated at losing my little baby. I hadn't grasped how devastated I was until Paula asked. We did some crystal work, some Reiki and some angel work. I felt surprisingly lighter by the end of the session. During our session Paula had asked me to think of my womb as a little place for a new baby to feel safe and that it gave a beautiful glowing light. After the session I really felt I had to tell Paula that my womb was glowing orange and how strange that was. Why on Earth would it glow that colour? Paula explained that was the colour of the corresponding chakra. I never knew this so it highlights how intuitive you can be.

I visited Paula regularly and got a lot of benefit from our sessions. I had studied angels and looked into their abilities more. I had my own cards and was using them regularly, but I hadn't seen my own angel. Angels were helping me a lot with my business (I still have my Archangel Michael card protecting my shop) and with my personal life.

One night I was in bed with my husband, when I woke up. It was half daylight. I looked up to see John (my husband) kneeling above me on his knees. I kept looking at him, trying to focus on what he was doing, but it was a bit strange because it didn't look like him. In fact, I couldn't see a face. It was like someone with their head bowed above me. I put my hand out, thinking that I would grab John and make him lie down, but my hands didn't make contact with anything. I swiped again, and again nothing. I was totally confused. I started to sit up and my husband moved. To my horror he was lying beside me and it wasn't him kneeling above me. I looked up at the figure above me and it started to fade. I never saw a face but I noticed big wings carefully folded in behind the body. I thought that I was dreaming but I knew I was wide awake. The figure faded slowly until it wasn't there anymore. I sat up and thought about what had just happened. I wasn't scared and felt secure. I knew I had just seen my angel and that he or she was looking after me. On the other hand, my husband was completely freaked out when I told him what happened!

Not long after that I found out I was pregnant. My daughter is now 15 months old and extremely healthy and happy. My husband has listened patiently to all my angel stuff. He now carries a crystal. He even asked the angels to get him a job after being made redundant. Within four hours of the request he got a call offering him a job!

I'm not sure how interesting this little story is but it shows the life-changing and dramatic impact that letting angels into my life has had. In fact, just writing it down has been amazingly therapeutic. This is my story.

Carrie shared this fabulous story of her little brother, who was certainly touched by an angel. When something like this comes from a child so young, who can doubt it?

My little brother, Dean, was allowed to hang out with my cousins (all boys) for the first time when he was four years old. It might sound young, but they only lived a couple of miles away, and their parents, my auntie and uncle, were going to be home all the time. I couldn't really blame my mum and dad because they both had to go to work, and had run out of funds for childminders. Also, my cousin Colin, the eldest, was 15 and he swore he'd watch out for Dean if they decided to play outside. Of course, in hindsight, a 15-year-old has no conception of how fast things can go wrong or how fast a young child can move if he wants to!

Apparently they were playing in the barn and everyone seemed to be OK, but boys will be boys and I suspect things got a little rough for Dean and he must have hidden somewhere. The group decided to race off to the river and got so carried away they didn't notice that Dean didn't go with them, until they got there. Colin, concerned about the deep water, looked around to make sure Dean didn't go too close, and at that point discovered he was missing. Hoping to avoid getting into big trouble, instead of telling his parents right away Colin decided to search the barn. By the time he realized Dean was really gone it was almost dark, that sort of country dark that is pretty much pitch.

Of course my parents would have been scared to death if they'd known, but as no one had told them there was a problem, they had decided to have a quick nap until it was time for Dean to be fetched. They were woken by a knock on the door, and there stood Dean – all alone! It turned out that he'd walked all two miles in the dark, along lanes that were a playing field for 'boy-racers', and no one could believe such a little kid could do that safely, let alone not be scared, and yet Dean wasn't at all scared. He said that an angel had walked with him and carried him when he got tired. When asked what the 'angel' looked like, all he would say was, 'You know, like an angel!' as if we were all stupid.

We'll never know for sure who it was, but I think it was an angel. Why? Because our driveway had just been dug up to be concreted and the builders had laid sand all the way up it just before they left. We all went out to look and there wasn't a footprint to be seen on the pristine surface of the sand.

Rachel Keene, who is a therapist, agreed to share the wonderful story of her brother Simon. I'm very grateful that she and her mother allowed me to use this very personal account. This is a long story, but I've included it in its entirety because, understandably, Rachel did not want it edited or changed by me. This story is of course very precious to her.

> When my mum, Judy, was rushed into theatre for her baby to be delivered by emergency caesarean, she was warned that Simon, my brother, only had a 50/50 chance of surviving. During the operation it became clear that the umbilical cord had prolapsed and was wrapped tightly around his neck, starving his brain of oxygen. Simon wasn't placed in the special care unit, because as far as the hospital was concerned there was nothing to worry about, and Simon was allowed home after ten days.
>
> I owe pretty much all of what I do today to my brother, even though due to his severe epilepsy and cerebellar ataxia, he had a mental age of just three years old, right up to 1991, when he died in his sleep aged 16. When he had his first massive seizure and was rushed to hospital in the middle of the night, all I can remember is my dad carrying me to the car in my pyjamas, and the awful sense of panic coming from my parents. At the time they were told that this was just a febrile convulsion due to Simon having a high temperature, and that he should be fine.
>
> However, after this first seizure my parents noticed that Simon would occasionally go blank, as if in a trance, and this occurrence became more frequent. Doctors

refused to believe there was anything wrong, but now we know these were *petit mal* epileptic seizures. Still, my parents were told he could grow out of it. But one GP contradicted this and told my mum coldly and 'matter of factly' that Simon's condition would deteriorate more and more until he died an early death. My mum was completely traumatized and didn't know what to think or believe. Simon's fits were a few months apart by then, but mum had noticed he was always very unsteady on his feet, even when he was well.

Eventually, when Simon was seven, a specialist diagnosed him as having a second condition due to the brain damage at birth – cerebellar ataxia.

Cerebellar ataxia is a disorder of the nervous system which causes unsteadiness and a lack of co-ordination. It is a progressive disorder and can place unbearable stress upon the heart. It is very rare, with the group Ataxia UK estimating that only a few thousand people are affected in this country. Walking for sufferers can become increasingly difficult, and it eventually becomes necessary to use a wheelchair. There is currently still no cure for people with cerebellar ataxia. Family life was of course entirely about Simon as he had to be supervised 24 hours a day. Mum and Dad never got to spend time together, so on rare occasions we had babysitters provided by the Red

Cross to give them a break. I didn't know any different, so I was happy and had plenty of friends to play with. One of whom I will mention later…

Going out could be difficult sometimes; people would stare at us in shops and public places if we were out and about with Simon because he looked perfectly normal but was often in a buggy as he couldn't walk far. And he was often quite loud, much to our amusement. He was hilarious! Despite his challenges, he was an absolute joy to know, full of smiles and laughter most of the time. He was a beautiful child, inside and out. I know I'm biased, being his older sister, but he had the face of an angel, big brown eyes, long lashes, and a smile and roaring laugh that lit up a room. Once met, he was never forgotten, as his kisses and big hugs of affection were given freely to everyone who came to our house.

Simon looked a lot younger than his years and was on so much medication for the epilepsy, but it unfortunately didn't control the seizures very well. Sometimes he would have one fit and that would be it for the day, and other days he would go on to have up to 35 in succession, with just seconds between one fit ending and another start-ing. We would sit by his bedside and wait them out with him, cooling him down with a fan as his little body went through terrible physical punishment. He was so groggy between fits that on those days he just slept. Simon had no idea what was happening to him during or after the seizures, he had no idea what a seizure was ... and a few days later he would be back to his usual happy, contented self.

As far back as I can remember I knew the drill when Simon had a seizure. It was normal to me; after all I'd never known anything different. Simon needed 24-hour supervision as he could potentially have a seizure at any moment. I was under strict instructions not to get him overexcited when we played together, as too much running around and laughing could trigger a seizure, so we played hide and seek and I'd give him piggy-back rides and swing him round and round until we were dizzy.

My parents had to show me how to administer Valium to him when I was just 11 years old, in case of emergencies. We had to keep a diary of the times and duration of all the fits to show the specialists at Guy's Hospital, as due to the severity of his condition, Simon was a test case for new drugs. As he got older the fits increased in severity, number and duration. We just had to sit by and keep him safe while they happened.

When Simon died unexpectedly in his sleep, we were completely devastated. The previous day had been completely uneventful and he had been his usual happy self, playing with his tape recorder, scoffing cottage pie and biscuits in the evening. I had stayed up late finishing my college coursework; I was studying fashion and business at the time and was two weeks away from completing the two-year course. On my way to bed at 2 a.m. I looked in on Simon, who was quietly snoring away as usual. But less than three hours later my father was waking me, telling me Simon was gone. I refused to believe him, and ran to see for myself. My brother looked like he was asleep. The post-mortem stated there was evidence to show he had had a seizure (he had bitten his tongue), and so they put it down to epilepsy as cause of death.

I was only 19 years old and this was my first experience of death, my little brother. I had assumed up to now that when someone died, that's it; they were dead and gone forever. I had no spiritual beliefs, and was a sceptical person about psychics and mediums in general. Almost 100 people turned up to Simon's funeral to say goodbye, including teachers from his special school and friends he'd known. He'd touched so many people during his life.

A few weeks after Simon's death, strange things started to happen. I would smell lilies when there were none in the house, and would catch faint whiffs of the smell of his hair, and saw fast-moving shadows on the periphery of my vision. I would often feel like someone was standing beside me or behind me when I was alone in the house.

I assumed it was all part of the grieving process and put it down to lack of sleep and round-the-clock crying, my senses playing tricks on me. More happened each day, but I tried to dismiss it all.

A few months later Simon made his presence really known. I was watching TV and from the corner of my eye saw a shadow travel across the floor from the doorway to the hall. When I looked directly at it I saw it was moving toward me. I kept blinking; I thought it was something in my eye, or my imagination ... then I could smell him, and when I asked for a sign that it was him, I felt a cold hand on my hand. I couldn't work out how I knew, but I just felt it was his energy. I wasn't scared, either – a bit freaked out, but I just knew it was him. And then in a moment he was gone again.

I think that was when I had to accept that there was an afterlife. I trusted what my own senses were telling me, that Simon had contacted me, and I wanted to know more about where Simon could be and what was happening to him in this other place.

I went along to a spiritualist church, and although their approach wasn't for me, I found it comforting to hear messages from this other place bringing comfort to some of the audience.

I had accepted there was an afterlife, but when a friend of mine asked me to go to a medium with her as 'the voice of reason', I agreed, and was ready to be the sceptical one, just in case this medium was a fraud. So when Rose, the medium, began reading my friend but kept being drawn to speaking with me instead, I felt a bit uncomfortable. She told me a few things I'd told no one. She stopped speaking at one point and told me I had a light across my eyes, and that it was because I should develop my ability and that I would be a better medium than her one day. I just laughed it off, but she insisted I hold her wedding ring, look into a candle flame and tell her what I saw and felt.

I don't to this day remember what I said; it was as if I went blank … but ten minutes later she said I'd just told her things that she hadn't even told her husband. Once again I laughed it off, as I was a bit unnerved by what had just happened.

I began speaking to other mediums and reading every psychic publication I could find. Publications were few in the early 1990s, and a lot of mediums weren't interested in passing on any development advice, but I persevered and found the information I needed to enable my spiritual learning.

A little later, the internet became an amazing source of information and put me in touch with other mediums, who were happy to share development advice with me. I practised and learned how to develop my psychic, clairvoyant and mediumistic abilities. I learned how to read tarot and auras. I worked with crystal healers and Reiki healers.

I pursued all of this in my spare time; I had gone from working in fashion to the travel industry, to working as a housing officer for a London borough. I kept it quiet that I was a medium, trusting only a select few. My family were, shockingly, very supportive when I 'came out' as a medium! I discovered that both my grandmothers had showed clairvoyant streaks, though they never would admit it! I was very wary and still am sceptical about a lot of things I hear and read. Just because I believe in my own experiences does not mean I blindly believe in everything under the paranormal umbrella. I learned to trust myself and found I just 'knew' things, so I began keeping a journal to record thoughts and meditation experiences, and found that a lot of things I saw did come to pass, or that my instincts were right further on about situations or people I had just met.

Simon popped in from time to time when I did my daily meditations, and introduced me to my first spirit guide. Now I have four! One is my doorkeeper, one is my healing guide, one turns up when he feels like it and one has always been with me for general guidance. When Simon or my guides came to me in meditation I acquired new knowledge about who we all really are. I was amazed that Simon could speak eloquently and was quite unemotional yet spiritual about how he had suffered in his short life, and didn't mind that he had gone back to Spirit so young in our concept of time.

I was shown over the years that we choose if, when and how our lives are lived on the Earth plane, and that Simon had chosen a life of physical and mental challenge because he wanted to know what it was to walk a mile in those shoes, to gain understanding to help others. We all do this, no matter how hard the life we choose to live. It really helped me to come to terms with losing loved ones as time went on. I know we would all meet again one day. Simon also showed me that we all choose purpose and roles in the Spirit world, and that his true role in Spirit at present is as a 'spiritual paramedic' – greeting and counselling those who cross back to Spirit suddenly and helping them to readjust to life on the other side.

In 1999, my life was changed forever when I fell down some stone steps. I sustained a serious leg injury which required two emergency surgeries to repair the bones and soft tissues. I was unable to work for three months; I was on crutches for over a year. To this day I can't drive or walk far. Unable to get about in those first months at home after the surgery, I built a website dedicated to Simon's memory, and my psychic experiences since losing him. I started to write and found I knew a lot more than I realized, and wanted to share it with people who might find themselves in the same confusing situation when their own psychic ability comes to the fore. Starting the website (which is now over 120 pages) gave me a distraction at a very low time for me, and a purpose for the rest of my life as the e-mails I receive, and the readings and advice I give now help so many people all over the world.

I know Simon had a hand in bringing me and my fiancé together, because I would never have been in the place we met in 1992, had Simon still been here. There are so many other synchronicities that would have drawn me and John together in time, all of which happened after Simon crossed over, and so my path was changed again.

I am sure Simon came to save me in September 2000. John was driving us to work in our car; it was a rainy morning and we were on a dual carriageway when a car spun out of control across both lanes of the carriageway in front of us. There was another car between us and the spinning car, and our brakes locked, the car skidding across the wet road for what seemed like an age, although the whole thing lasted just seconds. I was stupidly not wearing my seatbelt, and remember just closing my eyes and thinking, *Oh no, what a shame, I had so much more to do!* I was 28 years old, and in those seconds I felt sure I was about to die. We slammed into the back of that car still travelling at 45mph, according to the speedometer afterwards.

John, being the wonderful man he is, threw his arm across me as far as he could when he realized we were going to crash, but it was hopeless, the force was too strong and I flew out of my seat ... straight toward the windscreen. I could so easily predict what hitting it with my face was going to do to me. It was inevitable. Time seemed to slow down, and then I suddenly felt a powerful arm pushing me back against the passenger door side. It made no sense; it was completely against the laws of gravity, but I know I felt that arm! The car was a complete write-off. John was fine, no injury at all, but he had to kick his way out of the door as the engine had been pushed so far back into the car. When we saw just how bad the damage was afterwards, engine obliterated, car twisted ... we both knew we had been saved.

I plucked up the courage to do my spiritual work full time in 2005. My health was poor, I couldn't bear the daily grind of working in an office, I was under pressure from my employer due to my health and I just had a moment of clarity – why was owning a house and clinging to material things so important? Would the world end if I let them go? What could I do to make our lives happier? After a talk with my fiancé, we agreed it was nonsense clinging to things that brought us no happiness, and we decided to sell up and move to the country so I could do my work in peace and quiet and not have to worry about making ends meet. We realized we could survive on very little if we had to, and so we sold or gave away a lot of our material things in order to make it happen. In 2006 we finally moved to a tiny cottage in a rural village, and have never been happier!

As good old synchronicity would have it, Rose, the medium who first told me I had ability, came back into my life in 2005, when I provided a reading for a man who was a member of her paranormal group. He had no idea I knew of Rose; he chose me to do a reading because he was drawn to me, having found my website. He could have chosen any of the thousands of online mediums out there. Was he guided to choose me? I believe so. It was only when we were chatting about paranormal investigation at the end of the reading that it became apparent we both knew Rose, as she was his group's medium! I told him how Rose and I met, and asked him to pass on my regards to her.

Rose got in touch with me within a week and we became good friends. It was like coming full circle for me; the final seal of approval from Spirit that I was on the right path for life now. I know it was meant to be that we met again, as she died shortly after in early 2006. She told me soon after we met again that I had made her very proud by choosing this path, and that if she died tomorrow she would die a happy woman knowing she had helped to set me on this path in some small way. I never thought she would leave so soon, but it was her time. She has been in touch since she crossed over, so I know she is fine and still has her great sense of humour – she made a camera start up on its own on a paranormal investigation in October 2006, and when we reviewed the video footage days later, we heard her voice on tape faintly saying, 'Rachel, it's me!' just before the camera incident! I will never forget her or the comfort she brought me after Simon died, before I ever knew I was a potential medium.

These days I do a lot of different things, as over the years I have learned everything I can as new opportunities to do so come along. We never stop learning. I am now a fully fledged clairvoyant medium, exorcist, psychic artist (I can draw people's spirit guides) Reiki healing practitioner, an ethereal crystal therapy master, a past-life regression therapist and writer. I spend my days providing readings, healings and regressions, and my nights are often spent in a haunted location as I now work with paranormal investigation team Haunted Realms, too, as one of the founder members.

In very recent times I've made a few 'hindsight' discoveries which have shown me that I have had the ability since birth, as we all do to varying degrees.

I was talking with my mum last year about the street where we used to live until I was four. I asked her about Rebecca, the girl I remembered from a few doors down, who would play with me on the swing in our garden when I was three or four years old. My mum had no idea who I was talking about! But Rebecca is one of my most vivid early childhood friends; memories of her were part of my childhood! How could my mum not know her? She was in our garden all summer with me!

I knew she lived a few doors away on our cul-de-sac, and we would giggle and laugh on the swing! I realized quickly that this was a spirit child, because when I really thought about it, I couldn't remember ever pushing her on the swing or touching her ,.. just that she was there in the same dress each time…

My mum also has an embarrassing habit of getting out my old childhood drawings and poems from when

I was ten or 11 and showing them to my fiancé, much to his mirth! Last year Mum found another batch of my drawings tucked away somewhere ... but this time I was intrigued, not embarrassed. These were drawings of two faces with names. I had forgotten that I would often be prompted to draw faces or whole people, name them and give the drawing to a specific person. I had no idea why and it baffled me slightly at the time, but I went with it. Looking back, I believe this was when I was first subconsciously prompted to draw spirit guides for people.

I love my life, and I owe it all to Simon. I now know he and I agreed a shared purpose before we decided to come to this life, to shine a light into dark places ... and thanks to his choices, I am able to carry on the good work!

I know, as many other people know, that children like Simon and children with other disabilities or problems are very special indeed. They come into their often short lives on the wings of an angel, and they leave the same way, leaving their loved ones bereft and changed by having known them. They are real miracle workers, teachers and wonderful examples to the rest of us.

MOST IMPORTANT FACT

Children have a natural and intuitive connection to
their angels, so never ridicule anything your children
may say about their angel friends.

CHAPTER 6

Does Your Pet Have an Angel?

Every living thing on the planet has angels of some sort watching over them. From soul angels who watch over souls from their most primitive stage, when they are just a spark in the soil, up through their plant and animal stages and right through to their human incarnation, to master path angels who steer and guide us to our right path in our human lives. So of course our pets have angels, too.

My favourite quote from the Bible is from Job 12:7–10, and it says, 'Ask the animals, and they will teach you.' In many ways animals are more spiritual than humans. They are attuned to instincts that we once had but have allowed to atrophy. They never discriminate between animals of a different colour. They are more closely connected to Nature, and therefore God, than we are, and in my opinion the domesticated ones have agreed to live with us so that we can learn from them. Humans are not the pinnacle of the physical world as some people like to think. Human form is just the last and hardest test we have to face as mortals. And if we didn't experience being animals before we became humans, we would have no chance at all of sustaining spirituality in our human form, up against all the moral dilemmas, temptations, fears and desires that come with being human. Animals are vital to the planet and to our spiritual journey in so many ways that to deny them having the same access as we do to angels would verge on the ridiculous. It behoves every one of us to treat animals kindly and to instil trust in them, for they are to become human one day, and they can never become what they fear. In this way we carry a great responsibility for the progression of their souls.

DEVOTION

Some animals and pets demonstrate their closeness to angels with extraordinary devotion to duty, such as Chocolat, a Belgian Shepherd army dog, who was reported in national newspapers as showing an obsession for his job of saving lives. In Operation Moshtarak in Afghanistan, he refused to leave a building that the soldiers had cleared as safe, insisting that his handler went back into the area with him. Chocolat's handler then discovered enough explosives for ten bombs.

ANGELIC COMPASSION

Kathleen told me this story of a dog that was surely inhabited by an angel.

My stepson Andrew's father-in-law passed last spring. We took care of Andrew's daughters when they went back to Illinois for the funeral. Now, his widowed mother-in-law, Carolyn, has left her home in Illinois and moved here to Port Orchard. She and her late husband had been planning to move here, before he passed suddenly from a massive heart attack following major surgery. She felt she was doing what he wanted her to do by coming here. She's here now with her daughter (Andrew's wife), dealing with the loss of the love of her life. Carolyn brought the dog that had belonged to both of them with her. He's a white dog, named Polar Bear. She feels that the spirit of her late husband is there in the dog to comfort her. When she told me about this, it reminded me of a movie I saw years ago called *To Dance with the White Dog*. The story was based on actual events in the life of the author, and is about a man whose wife passes away suddenly and then appears as a white dog who becomes his close companion and guardian, and that he feels contains the spirit of his late wife. Anyway ... I have ordered the DVD of this movie for Carolyn. I will be giving it to her soon to watch, as I told her about it. She feels strongly that her husband's spirit is there in the dog. The problem now is that the dog has a severe heart problem. Her husband passed because of a severe heart problem. What are your thoughts on helping Carolyn through all this?

My feelings are that Carolyn could be right. The form of a white dog or wolf has been used by angels many times to bring comfort to people who have lost someone. I feel that Carolyn may be too upset and her emotions too turbulent for her energy to allow her husband to contact her directly, so why not, with angelic help, through their dog? I feel that, sadly, the dog will also pass suddenly from the heart problem, but this too, if she chooses or is able to accept it, will be a message of sorts to Carolyn. It will be that heart problems are transitory and they too will pass as will the physical bodies. Love, however, goes on.

PETS WHO CAN'T BEAR TO LEAVE

Then you get the pets that pull every string they can with their soul angels so that they can come back to their owners in a new body after they die. Alice Jean has become one of the closest friends I've never met (yet, or in this life) and she's shared yet another amazing story with me. I would never have found her if not for writing my book, *Pets Have Souls Too.*

The first week of September something else was added when a friend, Renee, e-mailed several on her list to say that her friend, Gigi, had to find a home for two cats that her mother couldn't take to the nursing home. (Gigi and her husband are trying to move out of state with their dog and two cats.) There was a photo included but I didn't look at it. I didn't even look because I was saying in my head, 'No. We don't need two more cats.' They were a neutered male and a spayed female that had been together all their lives and were about ten years old. Both were black and white. 'She'll be OK and find them a home,' I told myself. Hubby came home from work and asked me if I got the e-mail from Renee and did I look at the photos. He pulled it up on his computer to show me, and I couldn't take my eyes off one of them especially. He looked familiar to me but I didn't want to think about it. I did e-mail this to Gigi, and told her not to worry, that I would also ask around and if it came down to it I'd foster them at least. Then it all began! Gigi and I e-mailed each other and couldn't get over the synchronicities in our lives. I wish I could send you all those e-mails – they're unbelievable! Then I said we'd come to get the kitties as the month was running out and they'd had no other offers. My knees were really hurting that day so I sat downstairs while hubby went up with Gigi and John to put the two cats in the carriers, so I didn't see their faces til they were put in the car. Before I got in the car I peeked in on them and when I looked into the eyes of the male, for some reason I found myself asking him, 'Is that you?' He answered me with a one-syllable meow. I almost started to cry right there. I just knew he was my big male black and white Smudgie, who had died many years before. I had loved him so much and he had loved me. He was so big and such a happy guy til the day he got sick. The vet did all kinds of blood work, etc. in an effort to save him, to no avail, and was sure he had gotten into some kind of poison. I figured that in a few days I'd know for sure if the new cat was the one I'd lost. I needed a good sign. It only took a day. I was about to open my eyes the first morning they were there when I felt a cat jump on the bed. A 22-pound cat! I kept my eyes closed as I felt him making his way up toward the pillows. I was on my right side, with my arm and hand on the middle pillow as I felt him hoist his weight just right to where he wanted to settle. Then I got my sign ... he put his head in my hand! Total déjà vu! It surprised me so much I didn't move a muscle. I just opened my eyes to see that he had his head tilted up so that I could see that faint black smudge under his chin. My kitty that died of kidney failure many years ago had this smudge (not a patch of black fur) slightly larger in the same place, and got named Smudgie the day he was born. Oh, and Gigi's mother had named him Angel Kitty.

The female, who is not his litter mate, is Abigail and so sweet! She acts as if she knows me and I'm trying to figure her out. She came to my side of the bed the first night they were here, meowing and rubbing on the bed. I got up and picked her up and she purred, so I put her on the bed and she stayed.

It's always really good when we get a physical sign that a pet has returned. It's a wonderful thing when a pet will go through so much to get back to you. And with a little angel help, it usually works out that they make it.

VOICES OF A HEAVENLY HOST

Fausteen sent me this beautiful story about the devotion between two pets, and the incredible sound that heralded their departure from this life and their reunion in the afterlife.

Before our daughter was born, my husband came home one day with two ginger kittens and they were delightful. We named them Brownie and Goldie after the colour of the collars they wore. When they were about 18 months old, Brownie went missing. I received a call at work;

a kind stranger (or angel, maybe?!) told me they had removed Brownie's collar from the corpse they'd found on the roadside and were thus able to pass on this sad news. That evening Goldie and I were in the kitchen, both looking toward the window. Goldie let out a sound I had never heard before or after, and turned his head to me with profound sadness.

Goldie remained with us for another ten years until, finally, he got sick. He spent a night at the vet's but, knowing he was dying, I brought him home. He painfully made his way upstairs, calling out to our daughter and not finding her in her room, then settling down in the passage to wait. When she returned with her dad, Goldie was 'travelling', his breathing had the death rattle and he could barely move. We were having our bedroom re-modelled and were sleeping in the lounge, but I remained with Goldie and our daughter in her room until the small hours. Eventually, I crept downstairs.

Some while later I awoke to music. Beautiful, indescribable music ... Startled, I thought it was the radio-alarm clock above in our bedroom and I roused my husband and asked that he go check. He reported that the radio-alarm was unplugged, however Goldie had passed. The music I heard? It was the heavenly host greeting our much, much loved pet home.

HEALING YOUR PET

Now that you know that your pet has angels just as you do, there are ways to call on their soul angel to help them in times of need. But you must always consult a vet if you feel your pet has a health problem. All the healers I've worked with use angelic energy in their work. When you're carrying out this kind of healing you must always state your intent of working with the highest energy for the animal's best welfare. It has to be accepted that sometimes we just have to let our pets go, but healing can work miracles, as you will see.

HANDS-ON HEALING

Animals seem to love hands-on healing, and once they get used to it they will often go into a sort of trance. To do this, first get your pet comfortably settled within your reach. Close your eyes, letting your calm energy travel to your pet, as this will help keep them still while you get started. Call upon your angels to bring healing power down through the top of your head, and visualize it there, pouring down like concentrated golden rain from the universe. Place your hands over your pet and, gently stroking them, allow the golden light to pour from your hands into your pet. They may fidget for a few moments, as they will definitely feel something unusual going on, but they will settle and start to bask in the energy. The reason you must do this through angels is that if you just poured your own energy into your pet, you could well drain yourself, and you might even accept your pet's problem into your own body.

My husband Tony is a fully-trained and qualified spiritual healer. Recently, our lovely dog KC had a lameness problem. It started (or so we thought) about a year ago, when she was lame on her right front leg intermittently. Of course we took her to the vet's, but he couldn't see anything at the time and an examination didn't reveal any problems. Soon the lameness became worse, and before long she was lame every time she trotted. Back to the vet's we went. I was getting quite upset about this, of course, as she is a very lively dog and our main hobby is going for walks with her. It hurt to see her limping. The vet still couldn't find any obvious reason for her lameness but suggested a joint supplement. Unfortunately, KC has a very delicate tummy and the supplement upset it, so we couldn't continue. They didn't seem to be having any effect anyway. Soon she was lame even at a walk. It's funny how in situations like this, when we become afraid and anxious, we tend to veer away from spiritual solutions. I know that my energy was negative and afraid at the time and, like most people, I found it difficult to overcome for a while. I tried to communicate with her in my usual way to see what was wrong, but I couldn't get anything except 'my paw' and the vet couldn't find anything wrong with her paw. KC went for X-rays and my fear increased as the vet said that as well as myriad nasty problems such as arthritis, he'd be looking also for bone cancer.

Thanks goodness the X-ray didn't show anything at all. This was good in many ways, but it still left us dangling with no cause to work on. We decided to take KC for hydrotherapy as we'd heard of good results from this. Still, Tony hadn't tried healing her, because we had no idea where the root of the problem was and we were too upset to focus. Anyone who's read any of my other books knows what KC means to us. My angels must have been tearing their hair out by now! We took her and it was good and bad. The good part was that the physiotherapist who examined her and asked many questions seemed to be able to pinpoint the cause. During the answers we gave to her questions we told her that two years previously KC had cut her right paw quite badly on a sharp stone in a riverbed. She been treated by the vet and had been lame for about two weeks in all. The physiotherapist detected some instability in KC's right shoulder. She said that because dogs don't have a collarbone like us to hold their shoulders in place, they are held there purely by muscle power.

She said that because KC had been favouring her right leg (paw) for those two weeks, the shoulder muscles had become weak and prone to strain. She thought swimming might help.

We took KC into the pool area and handed her over to the hydrotherapist. It was a nightmare for the next five minutes. KC adores swimming, which was why she was in the river in the first place, so we weren't anticipating any problems. However, in this instance, after she was strapped into a lifejacket, three clips from suspended ropes were clipped on and KC was hoisted into the middle of the deep pool. She was terrified. Her eyes were bulging out and after a minute of her trying frantically to swim to the side of the pool, I could virtually hear her screaming in my head, 'What's wrong with you? Help me! I'm drowning!'

It was a traumatic experience for all three of us, and we were deflated because we'd hoped it might help but we couldn't put her through that again! It was on the way home that, sunk in the passenger seat, I started to get a handle on things – and because I did that, my angel was able to give me the answers as to what we should do. We should take her swimming ourselves as much as possible. The cold water would help, we were told. I knew I was on the right track because by the time we got home KC was quite a bit better. I was also told that Tony should heal her paw, which seemed a bit odd but as KC had also said 'paw', it seemed the right thing to do. I tried, at this stage, to put a pad under her paw but that seemed to make her lamer, which was interesting. Tony started intensive hands-on healing. Any time he had he'd sit by her and place his hands on her. She is used to the sensation and would settle down and enjoy the feel of the energy pulsing through her.

After a few days I noticed a little speck of white on one of her right pads. I tried to wipe it off but it wouldn't go. I had to pick it off with my fingernail and it left a tiny dent in her paw. It was so minute that as I picked it off it vanished before I could get a close look at it. I mentioned it to Tony but we had no idea if it meant anything. A week or so later another white speck appeared, and again I had to pick it off. Again it left a deep dent. It wasn't like a bit of dirt or stone just clinging to her foot – it almost looked as if it had come *out* of her foot. Finally, the penny dropped! I could almost hear my angels groaning with relief! The little specks *were* stone and they *had* come out of her foot. They were tiny fragments of the point of the stone that had cut her – too small to show up on X-ray. They'd been trapped inside her pad for two years, gradually causing more and more pain. Tony's healing had drawn them to the surface. KC was completely sound within two more days. You can contact Tony through his page on my website.

Another hands-on healer is Lynne Statham, from East Sussex. She sent me this story about her healing of Mabel the cat for Mabel's owner, Anita.

Mabel is a beautiful five-year-old British Blue cat. Anita, her owner, bought her when she was three years old, after she'd had two litters of kittens. She was as small as a kitten herself when Anita went to see her. The breeder said she was selling Mabel because she couldn't keep any more cats in the house.

When Mabel arrived at her new home she used the litter tray several times – at the time this was thought to be due to the stress of her moving to a new home. However, the next day there was blood in the tray, and this ominous sign continued on a daily basis. Then there were times when she didn't use the tray at all. She also bolted her food and then very often vomited.

Anita took Mabel to the vet. He agreed that the symptoms could be due to stress and advised on diet. However, after a month with no improvement and, in fact, deterioration, Anita returned to the vet. He diagnosed colitis, and thought that Mabel had had this condition for a long time. He suggested this could be due to an overgrowth of bacteria in her gut or to a food intolerance. Mabel's diet was addressed again and she was given antibiotics over nine months. This initially helped, but gradually the symptoms returned. At this stage, Anita called me to ask if I might help Mabel. Anita had recently lost her husband and the situation was causing her additional stress, too.

When I arrived at the house I took off my coat and sat down on the settee. Mabel came into the room, jumped onto the settee and lay down on my coat. This meant I was able to easily give her 'hands-on healing', which she accepted happily, and in fact she dozed off. Although I'm often asked to give healing just to an animal, I like to give healing to the owner as well if they are agreeable. They have a partnership and their energies are closely connected, and so I gave Anita healing, too.

As a healer my intention is to be a healing channel for the natural universal healing energy, and send out love to the animal unconditionally for its higher good, without any expectations of the outcome. A cure cannot be promised, but I believe no limitations should be set either. The animal will receive the healing needed at that time.

Healing can sometimes be successful after one treatment, depending on the condition. As Mabel's condition was chronic, I gave her healing every month. The length of time I spent healing Mabel lessened as she improved. Animals will dictate the length of time needed for healing by getting up, moving around or becoming restless after previously being in a relaxed state. There are times when they may not need any healing at a particular time.

I continued to visit once a month over the next year, giving healing to Mabel, who continued to improve. Mabel has now put on weight, is eating well and is not bolting her food. Her toilet habits are now impeccable with no sign of blood. I still have continued to give Anita healing each time I visit, which I continue to do because healing is beneficial for the maintenance of good health.

Mabel is now symptom-free, and she and Anita are enjoying a happy and healthy partnership.

PAST-LIFE TRAUMA HEALING

If, when you're connected angelically to your pet in this way, you start to get pictures in your mind's eye, then your angel is showing you what has caused your pet's problem in the first place. All sorts of problems can be addressed in this way, from illnesses to behavioural problems. When you piece together the visions you should be able to understand an event that took place in the past, maybe as far back as a past life. Let it run like a video in your mind. Then concentrate on changing the sequence of events to a happy outcome. This is called rewriting the script, and there are people who do this professionally if you don't feel able. One such person is Madeleine Walker from Taunton in Somerset. She sent me this amazing and dramatic account of one of the animals she treated this way.

I was called out to a livery yard and met a lovely horse called Seamus. He was a beautiful dappled grey and he stomped nervously, snorting through his flared nostrils as I gently tried to reassure him that I was there to help. He had some fears about being loaded into a horsebox and some confidence issues with his ridden work. However, I discovered that although these issues were very real to him, there was a much deeper reason for his behaviour and that he was indeed fearful, but also very worried about a chestnut horse that really needed my help. I checked this piece of information with his owner and she said she thought he might be referring to her daughter's horse, Raj. However, she said that her daughter Mary and Raj were away at the time but that this horse was becoming increasingly unpredictable and that she was worried for her daughter's safety at times. We discussed the emotional healing that I would perform for Seamus and perhaps some remedies that my veterinary friend could prescribe, and agreed that when Raj and Mary came home I would visit and see if I could help. I subsequently got a call a few weeks later. I entered the barn where the horses were stabled. I was greeted by Seamus who, I swear, winked at me and pointed with his head in the direction of a large chestnut horse at the end of the barn and said, clear as day in my head, 'For goodness' sake, sort them out! They've got real issues.' I thanked Seamus for his help and said telepathically that I would do my best. I was eyed a little suspiciously by Raj as I neared his box. He was a very large and powerful horse and Mary looked rather diminutive next to him as she held his halter rope. Mary described some of the problems she had been having with Raj, how he had lost his confidence and that he seemed to have a real issue with turning to the left. When I questioned Raj in my mind, connecting telepathically with him, he said that he needed Mary to be more confident in herself, so that she could be a stronger leader for him. If she believed in him, he could then believe in himself. I then noticed a large splash of much darker fur on his right shoulder, surrounded by a white outline. When I asked Mary about it, she said that she had been told that he had been born with the large mark and that there had been no injury to his shoulder as far as she was aware. I felt there were bells going off in my head and I tuned in to the energy of the shoulder. I asked Raj to show me what was going on and if this was the cause of his concerns. In the past I have been asked to remove energetic 'foreign objects' from a past-life wound, and in that moment I was 'shown' pieces of shrapnel-like metal, embedded as a memory within Raj's shoulder. I wondered how I was going to explain this to Mary and her mother, who were watching my strange actions as I visualized removing energetic pieces of metal. They must have wondered what on Earth I was doing as I physically plucked what looked like thin air out of Raj's shoulder, and then I visualized filling the area with healing light. Mary then started to feel a stabbing pain in her left shoulder. I described as gently as I could the video-like clip that Raj was running through my mind. I was being shown a past life in a Napoleonic battle. I could see Raj as a powerful grey horse and Mary as a soldier on his back, charging through a battlefield in the midst of cannon fire. Mary, as a man, had her sabre raised, but unfortunately they were hit broadside as a cannon exploded next to them and metal flew into Raj's shoulder, throwing them sideways onto their left sides. Sadly the wounds were too serious for Raj to survive, and Mary, though crushed beneath the dying horse, somehow managed to survive the battle. She sustained severe injuries that left her with a withered arm and a much weakened left side.

Mary was a little perplexed at the increasing pain she was feeling in her arm and her mother probably thought that I was deranged, and was probably wondering what had possessed her to call me out in the first place! I worked to remove the negative memory in Mary's arm and I asked her if she could imagine the scene that Raj had shown me – to her amazement she was able to describe every detail of her uniform and how they both looked in that lifetime. Mary's mother was also astonished, but I'm sure still wondering where this was all leading. I knew that Mary was really feeling the past-life trauma in her body, and could feel tingling as though something was changing in her arm. She then disclosed that she had always been very weak in her left arm, and in fact her whole left side was much the same way and that she had experienced difficulty in steering and controlling Raj because of the weakness in the left side of her body. I felt this attributed to his difficulty in turning to the left. She then said that she felt that, somehow, the renewed energy in her arm had become a little blocked at the elbow, so I asked Raj to help me to clear it. He had become very quiet and totally focused on the proceedings, and was working so hard to support Mary through the process, it was almost as though he was fixing her with his gaze, willing her to continue in order to finally release their trauma. I was guided to ask Mary to visualize little taps at the ends of her fingers that we could open, in order to allow the old blocked energy to be released. I pretended to turn imaginary taps on each finger and asked Mary's permission to hold her hand between mine, so that I could facilitate the release of the old stuck energy. I visualized dark, treacle-like energy coming out, and asked Mary what she would like to transmute it into.

Amazingly, she said that she could imagine little daisies floating skyward, taking all the trauma away. She also visualized the pain in her shoulder leaving and turning into daisies, which carried away the pain. She also felt a block in her head, which she released by blowing daisies out of her mouth. I thought this was very interesting, as the homeopathic remedy for deep tissue trauma can be *Bellis perennis*, which comes from the Daisy plant. I then asked Mary to visualize changing the outcome of the battle, where this time maybe they could dodge the cannon fire and gallop to safety. This she did with the help of Raj as she described the emotions of fear, but also the relief at escaping, unscathed, from the battle. Suddenly Mary went white as a sheet and she exclaimed that she felt very sick. She looked as though she was about to pass out, so I suggested that she sit down. She slid down the stable wall and sat in a heap, looking alarmingly pale. With that Raj gave a huge sigh and almost collapsed onto the straw. His eyes were tightly closed and his muzzle was pressed on the floor as he snorted and groaned. I was rather alarmed, as I had never experienced quite such a dramatic response from either horse or owner before. However, I knew that it was just such a huge energetic shift in their cell memories and that they just needed time to adjust to their new way of being. I guided Mary to take some deep breaths and to allow herself to rest. We visualized the new tingly energy filling her whole left arm and when it reached her fingertips we imagined turning off the taps to seal in all the new healing energy. Eventually the colour started to return to Mary's cheeks and she felt strong enough to stand. Raj was still out for the count and breathing heavily. I felt he had worked so hard to help Mary and himself release the past that he, too, had needed to just 'flop' in order to recover and adjust to his new energy. I felt that Mary needed to get back to the house and have a warm drink. Her mother and I gently led her up the yard to the house and, amazingly, Mary began to smile. She almost shouted that her whole left side felt different – stronger somehow, much to her mother's amazement. When she was handed a mug of tea once inside the warm kitchen, there was more commotion. She shouted in amazement that she could actually squeeze her mug. She had never been able to make a strong fist with her left hand. Her mother was incredulous, but the evidence was there in front of us. Mary proudly demonstrated her tight fist that she was now able to make, and practised several times as if to convince herself of the amazing change in her physical ability. I was so thrilled, but still a little concerned about Raj, so we tiptoed down into the barn to make sure he was OK. As we passed Seamus, he said, in my head, 'Thank goodness, about time!' There, at the end of the barn, nonchalantly leaning over his stable door was Raj, cool as a cucumber, looking as though nothing had happened. His eyes were calm and he seemed really happy and relaxed, which was very different to when I had arrived. I finally felt confident to leave them both, as I felt they were settling into their new personas, having released all the past that was so limiting to them both. I advised Mary to rest herself and Raj as much as possible over the next couple of days and to let me know how they were feeling and give feedback on their progress. I had several other calls to make with horses in the area and wondered what I would be confronted with next on my day's adventures. The other cases were all interesting and rewarding, but the case with Mary and Raj had been so dramatic, with instant results. I was totally blown away by the chain of events that had led me to working with them both. I felt that Seamus, in his wisdom, had decided to get this sorted once and for all so had possibly exaggerated his behaviour in order that I might be called to rectify it and then the real pressing issue of Mary and Raj could finally be healed.

The feedback was fantastic. Seamus was loading beautifully and was a very happy 'bunny'. Mary and Raj were literally going from strength to strength, giving each other so much confidence that they were finally able to bond completely as a team for their combined equestrian endeavours.

Madeleine has often amazed me with her work, but that one is probably my favourite story.

DISTANCE HEALING

One of the most interesting things about animal healing is that there's no place for the placebo effect. This is especially relevant in distance healing, when the healer and the animal don't make direct contact. If direct contact is made then a sceptic might easily say that the healer is just a very good person with animals, and that the animals might just be responding very strongly to their presence. I'm quite aware that this isn't so. The truth is rather that people who are very charismatic to animals often use this natural ability to get close enough to the animal, and be trusted enough, so that spiritual exchange between them might take place. The placebo effect in essence means that if you tell someone that a certain pill or action is going to improve things for them, then often it *will* have that effect. It works very well when people are given a pill that they think holds a powerful drug, and it works as if it does, even though in fact the pill is nothing but sugar. Of course with animals what you see is what you get, and the animal cannot be 'told' that the treatment it receives will help it. In distance healing there is no expectation at all on the part of the animal. Unlike a human patient, it can't be told to expect healing at a certain time, so whatever happens must therefore be a genuine result of the treatment.

These are just two examples of distance healing from the amazing Rosemary Lee.

Arielle was a lovely whippet dog who had a severe mitral valve prolapse. In the sonogram you could see the prolapsed valve and the blood pouring back through the valve. The prognosis was bad. She was being treated with homeopathy, but her owner wasn't convinced she was on the right remedy. She contacted me after Arielle had a particularly bad night. Her breathing was up around 60 breaths a minute (for dogs, ten to 30 breaths is normal). She was on Lasix, a diuretic, to clear the fluid out of the lungs, but it didn't seem to be working very well. Her appetite was down and she was underweight. Her owner was very worried about her.

This was the communication from her owner after the first distance-healing session had been done:

'I just wanted to tell you that Arielle is doing much better. She has both her energy and her appetite back. I took Arielle and Lily (my other whippet) to the park yesterday and Arielle actually ran and romped! She hasn't done that in several weeks. She seems really happy and perky – the spark in her eyes is back. Her breathing is settling into the 20s (per minute). At one time her breathing was in the 50s, now it's in the 20s most of the time, which is within normal range. Thank you, thank you, thank you for the healings and advice.' Then there was a further update:

'This is good news! Arielle is doing very well. She has gained 1.4 pounds! Her appetite is very good, and 28.4 pounds is a very normal, good weight for a whippet. Her breathing is much better. I took Arielle and her sister Lily for hikes on Saturday and Sunday, and as always, I let Arielle set the pace. Her pace was actually normal! Usually when we go for walks it is extremely slow, and I have to tell myself, "This is a walking meditation," so I don't mind the slowness. But she was keeping up a good pace this weekend. There are a couple of uphill segments on our hike, and she didn't seem to need time to recover (although I made us stop, just in case). She seemed super happy and perky. Thank you ever so much for your help with Arielle; she really is doing well. I am very grateful.'

Rosy's owner wrote to say that their dog had been diagnosed with mass cell tumours throughout her body and had been given approximately one week to live. They asked that I perform a healing session for her as soon as possible. Rosy was a rescue dog, and is approximately seven years old. She was in pain and was extremely uncomfortable. This was her third bout with the tumours – she'd undergone two surgeries at two different times, and her owners really didn't want to put her through another bout of surgery. They had some brief success with homeopathy but thought it was probably too late for it to help much. She had three major tumours on her left back hip. The day they contacted me they'd been to the vet's and Rosy's X-rays showed that the tumours had spread to her lymph gland and were causing various blockages around her colon and pressing on her bladder. Blood work showed infection.

This was their response after healing had taken place:

'Thank you for your session yesterday. Rosy is on tramadol, given to us by the vet on Saturday to ease her pain, so it's hard to tell if she is in less pain due to the pills or from your session. I will say this, though: she seemed to rally yesterday somewhat. But last night was not good. Breathing was shallow and we were pretty sure the end was near. Now, this morning is a different story. She seems to be more alert. She ate, with my help, eliminated in the yard, and has been lying in her favourite spot all morning. We wanted to ask you if you would be able to do another session on her today.'

Of course I did another healing on Rosy, and this was the result:

'Rosy is doing so much better today. She seems to be more alert, less bloated, even walks around (a little). These last couple of days she wouldn't even do that. Her breathing does not seem to be as shallow. Rosemary, it's a good day for her.'

Next update:

'Let me tell you about Rosy today. I took her to our traditional vet on Thursday morning for a follow-up. The vet said that our goal now was to just keep her comfortable. For the last two mornings Rosy and I have gone for a little walk in the front. Yesterday morning I took Rosy in the front and she began walking the route we take to the park. She trotted on ahead of me, sniffing and peeing here and there. She was doing so well that I let her continue to the park, as it's not too far. She sniffed some more, greeted a dog that was in its backyard, and home we went. This morning was pretty much a replay of yesterday. She is not the sick dog I thought I was going to lose last weekend. We have a room for the dogs and they have their own beds; last night was the first night Rosy wanted to sleep in her bed and not in the bed we made for her in our room. I am cautious with her, try not to overdo things, and at the same time give her some of her life pleasures. You are a good woman, Rosemary, blessings to you and all that you have, all that you are.'

Next update:

'Good morning Rosemary. Rosy is doing wonderfully. We have gone for our full walks these past two days. The walks are about a mile. Her energy level keeps improving, and her body functions appear to be back to normal. She is happy once again, wagging her tail and being excited about her walks, and her ears perk up when we pass other dogs in their yards. She's alert and follows me from room to room, and sleeps in her own bed. The tumours on her leg appear to have shrunk in size, and she is not licking at them or seeming to be as bothered by them. Her coat is the best I have seen it for a long time. We are so grateful to have our Rosy back. A few of my friends came by the house to see her when she was so sick, to say goodbye, now they come by and are amazed by her. She got her toenails cut today and just two weeks ago I did not think we would be doing any more grooming for her. Thank you for your work. She is our miracle pet.'

This incredible example of distance healing was sent to me by Susan Grey, who lives in South Carolina.

In August 2007, Briony found my distance-healing website and contacted me in the hope that I could be of help to her cat, Willow, whose liver was failing and the vet was not giving her much hope. I checked in intuitively and determined which of the distance-healing processes I use would be of help to Willow, and let Briony know what I was getting. I explained that although I never know what will be the final results of the distance-healing work I do, I have seen a lot of miracles. Briony lives in the United Kingdom, and I am in the United States. Briony agreed to have me send Willow healing. Following is Willow's story, in Briony's own words.

'Thought I'd share the really good news about Willow! She had all her blood tests and her repeat liver scan yesterday. Her bilirubin level (the stuff that made her go yellow!) should be 12. Last week hers was 50 and it has now gone down to 20. With the other two blood tests they did, one is back within its normal range and the other is just outside it, but has also dropped back significantly since last week. Even better than that, though, her liver scan shows that her liver has gone totally back to its original size and with no obvious problems. I can't tell you how thrilled my husband and I are about this! Providing she doesn't relapse for some reason, then we only have to go back to the vet in two weeks' time for a check-up...

'Update: it's official! The cat's a miracle! I just thought I'd let you know the latest on my cat, Willow ... This week we were back at the vet for her normal annual check-up and booster shot. We saw the vet who had seen her when she first got sick, and he couldn't believe the change in her. She has put 5lb back on and is 100 per cent healthy old mog again! The vet said he has only seen a couple of cases where a cat has made a full recovery after being so ill, and that initially it looked as though Willow had liver cancer, which would have killed her in four to six weeks. In fact Willow has even started to chase our dog Holly! Take care and a final big thank you!'

I contacted Briony again in May 2010 to get an update on Willow so I could share her distance-healing story. I asked her also to share what the distance-healing process was like, on her end. Again, in Briony's words:

'How great to hear from you! Well, I'm very pleased to report that Willow, Holly and Ruda are all doing great. Willow is now 12 years old and is still the madam of the house and in good health. She has managed to fool both me and the vets for two years running by showing all the symptoms of having a thyroid problem, but her blood tests come back normal. Willow has an unusually large thyroid, for a cat anyway, so that tends to complicate matters! She still manages to astound the vets whenever she goes in, as they look at her history, see her liver failure problem and then can't believe that she is still alive, let alone as well as she is! I just smile to myself and quietly send my thanks to you every time that happens.

'As to how the healing went at my end when you sent it, I've been trying to think how best to describe it. After I asked you to go ahead and send healing to Willow, there was no amazing, sudden "light bulb" moment as to when she received it. I think I could best describe it as a very gentle, but immediate, improvement to her health. That first day she started to pick up and just kept going from strength to strength. As I said before, it was to the complete amazement of the vets, as they said they had expected her to pass away within six weeks of diagnosis. As you can see from the photo I've attached, she has certainly regained all the weight she lost when she was ill, plus a bit extra for emergency use!'

Thank goodness there are people like these who recognize that animals have souls and angels, and possess the compassion to help them. It makes me cry if I think too deeply about the way animals are treated by some people in the world, and how we in the UK might be going to return to hunting and killing foxes with dogs. If only the perpetrators of cruelty realized that they stand no chance of their own angels helping them in life while they are committing acts of barbarism against animals. I recently watched a video on the internet of a cat in Turkey who was filmed trying to resuscitate his partner who had been killed by a car. The cat tried to revive her for two hours, kneading her chest and abdomen with his feet and touching his nose to her nose. Anyone who could watch that and not believe that cats, and indeed all animals, have souls, defies reason.

MOST IMPORTANT FACT

Every living thing on this planet, and in fact the very
fabric of the planet, is connected and we all affect
each other whether we want to or not. We have to
learn to accept this and not treat man as if he
is above Nature.

CHAPTER 7

Why the Angels Might Not Reach You

You already know that purity of mind, producing positive energy, is necessary in order to connect with angels. But it also helps to have purity of body, too. Destructive behaviours can actually generate such a pool of negativity that any amount of subsequent good thoughts cannot change your energy enough to allow angels near. For an angel to reach a person who intensely physically abuses their body is like someone trying to dive to the bottom of a toxic ocean. Even angels can't do it. But there is hope, so don't despair. Sometimes an angel will throw you a lifeline, and then it's all down to you. These are some of the conditions I'm talking about, together with the testimonies of some very brave people.

DRUGS

Gwen kindly allowed me to use her story, but I have changed her name to protect her and her family.

It all happened so easily. I started out 15 years ago, just having a laugh with cannabis, and moved on from there, so imperceptibly that I didn't realize what was going on. I was ashamed of myself because my parents had made a lot of sacrifices to put me through university, and I'd done really well, but before I knew it I was stealing money to pay for more and more drugs. I don't need to elaborate. Anyone who's been hooked on drugs knows this painful story. I was at rock bottom, or so I thought. I'd run out of money. I'd been thrown out of my digs because I couldn't pay the rent and was squatting in a place that once I'd never have thought of even going into, let alone living in. It was reaching the point when suicide seemed like the only option, and then one day something extraordinary happened. I was hunting around the backs of shops looking for stuff to steal or food past its sell-by date that I could eat, and I saw a sack full of stuff outside an Oxfam shop. Someone had obviously left it as a charitable donation – well, I was the best charity I could think of, so I took it. Unfortunately someone had beaten me to it, and there wasn't anything of much use in there, but there was the torn-off cover of a book. It had a drawing on it of a beautiful, lit-up being, with wings. Of course as a kid I'd heard about angels in school, and seen Christmas cards and decorations featuring angels, but I'd never believed they were real and never thought about one in relation to myself. Nevertheless, there was something about the light in this drawing. It made me want to keep it, so I stuffed it into my pocket. That night, by the light of a burned down tea light candle I got the picture out. That was the night I was expecting to die. I didn't have anything to take, and withdrawal was starting to make me shaky. I thought I might as well die. I was sure my family wouldn't miss me as I'd been nothing but trouble for the past three years, so I thought dying was a good idea. But as I sat and looked at the picture, something clicked in my mind and I thought there just might be someone after all that I could call on for help. I went into a peaceful sleep and when I woke up the next day I was determined to escape from my self-imposed cage. That day I started to turn my life around, and my inspiration was the picture. I knew somehow, in my heart, that the angel in the picture would love me no matter what and would help me. During the next few painful months I used to look at the picture whenever things got too tough.

It was six months later that I started to get angel messages all over the place, from posters, TV ads, car number plates, you name it. And every one of them pointed to one place – 'home'. I was so scared. I thought that if my family rejected me, as I thought they would (and I didn't blame them), it would push me back onto the drugs. But I took my courage in both hands and called my mum. She cried. I cried. I'm not sure if she believed me at that point when I said I was clean, but she invited me to visit her. I did and I've never looked back. When my mum realized that I really had changed, she talked to all the family and they agreed to let me back in. I'm not going to let them down again.

DRINK

Of course the same things apply in the case of drink. Some people believe that a small amount of red wine can enhance spiritual connection, but I've seen no evidence of that. Rather, a small amount of alcohol can tend to make someone read a spiritual experience wrongly or even see one when it's not there. In the case of several people drinking together, it can generate a mild case of group hysteria. You can imagine several people in a room together, all comfortably enjoying alcohol-induced relaxation. It only takes one of them to say, 'I felt something, did you?' for other people in the same state to start imagining that they too feel something. Before you know it they've all had a 'spiritual' experience which on closer inspection would seem to have been generated by the power of suggestion. As Maureen's story shows, a clear mind is necessary in order to connect with angels for real.

People said I'd joined a cult, and in hindsight maybe they were right. I found myself under the spell of a woman I'll call 'Jane'. When you're desperate for a spiritual experience and really need to have something to cling to, it's easy to be drawn in by someone who appears full of confidence and is very charismatic and forceful. Jane would insist on meeting with everyone in her group, at first once a week and then it gradually came down to once a day. She'd split from her husband, doing very well out of it, and had a lovely house into which I was welcomed as if a family member. There were about 15 of us at this time and we all hung on Jane's every word. She'd told us that red wine would enhance and change our brainwaves, making them receptive to spirit. I didn't understand the scientific stuff she spouted at us but it all sounded very plausible and, let's face it, I wanted to be convinced. During our gatherings – and by then several of us lived in the house all the time – we felt like a big family. We felt like we had support and love, and an opportunity from which we couldn't walk away. We revelled in belonging. Each evening we'd drink the red wine and, sure enough, after a while things would start to 'happen'. It ended up where we all totally believed we were having nightly conversations with aliens. I can actually still hear those weird voices in my head if I try. Looking back, I feel there was an element of group hypnosis about it. It's the only way to explain it. Then one day when I was out alone, which was unusual, I met Clive. It was instant for both of us and I was so happy to have finally met someone wonderful. I couldn't wait to introduce him to Jane, my friend and mentor, but her reaction dismayed me. She was furious and, because he didn't want to join our group, she forbade me from bringing him to the house, and she tried to stop me seeing him altogether. One evening I committed the ultimate sin and went out with Clive, missing the meeting. I snuck back at about 2 a.m., realizing how ridiculous it was that here I was at 45, acting like a naughty teenager. I crept into the lounge area where the meetings were and discovered a horrifying sight. They were all drunk, plain and simple drunk. There wasn't anything mystical going on. They were all talking gobbledegook, and it wasn't in any way like the smooth, spiritual connection with other beings I'd thought it was. Jane alone was sober, and she sat there with a smug smile on her face that made me feel sick. It was like she was soaking up their energy. I honestly believe she was feeding on them in some way. Needless to say, I left there that night and moved in with Clive. I'm actually scared to go back there now. Since I left I've found that real, gentle angel communication is possible, and I do it all with a clear head!

DIET

Having a healthy diet works wonders for your body, but it can also work wonders with your energy. It's important to look at yourself holistically, because while the body might appear to be mortal unlike the soul, and therefore less important, it is, during each life, the envelope for the soul, and as such needs to be as pure as possible. We've become too reliant on convenience, and most of us of the current generation have been brainwashed into thinking certain things are good for us or acceptable as 'treats', when in fact many of them are actually slow poisons.

I was as guilty as the next person in using convenience foods, hailed as they had been as the best thing for taste as well as speed, and of eating the wrong foods for me as 'treats'. Of course, eventually I found out that convenience and taste came at a price, that price being the additives and additions which made them so appealing. When my husband Tony was diagnosed with cancer, it was a huge wake-up call, and when we also discovered that we were both allergic to cow's milk, it prompted a whole new way of living for both of us. Out the window went dairy, sugar and anything processed, as well as alcohol, and in came a new era of cooking from scratch with fresh, unadulterated produce. Not only did this sort out our health, Tony's cancer included, but it also heralded a period of huge spiritual growth for us. With a healthy body comes clarity of mind, and with a clear picture comes a visible pathway. With the vitality that comes from these you find the means to walk down that pathway. So, when you're trying to achieve the best that you can spiritually, it makes sense not to sully the soul's receptacle.

Eating the wrong things or eating too much generally pollutes the body, the soul's carrier. There's always a reason for any kind of eating disorder, and these reasons are almost always related to past-life experiences. For instance, someone who was once stabbed to death will often over-eat because subconsciously they think a layer of fat will protect them 'next time'. Or, if they were responsible for others who died from malnutrition in a past life, they will starve themselves to assuage the unnecessary guilt they feel. Of course, if in either case they have their past healed by having past-life regression, these reasons will disappear, a healthy life will follow and their energy will become clean, allowing connection to angels.

Smoking won't help a connection to angels, either. Anything you take into your body that is unnatural and bad for it will damage your ability to communicate with angels. If you're trying to give up smoking, please continue to do so, bearing all this in mind!

PROMISCUITY

This is of course a recognized dangerous way of being, what with all the health implications in our current time, and, like drink and drugs, hopping around from bed to bed, whether you're male or female, mixes up the emotions and therefore interferes with your energy. Loving sex between two people can enhance spirituality, because love creates positive energy like no other state of mind, whereas sex alone with no love is merely a carnal act. Actual promiscuity, where the sex is performed with many varied partners, is actually an addiction, as real as alcoholism or drug abuse. Any form of addiction must by its very nature take away from other aspects of the self, including one's spirituality. When people are promiscuous because they're desperately seeking love, they're only setting themselves up for more disappointment and a gradual and inevitable downward spiral.

Jennie shares her story, although I have changed her name to protect her privacy.

I was a sex addict. No other word for it. I had my chances at a stable relationship, but every time it could have happened I'd mess it up, run away, whatever you want to call it. It wasn't til I was 30 that I felt a real need to change my life, but I couldn't do it. Eventually someone suggested I go for past-life therapy, and I found out that I'd been abused by one man for 40 years in a previous life! No wonder I didn't/couldn't bring myself to trust any one man in this life. I think I was also punishing myself, because, like most battered wives, I guess, I felt that I had to be to blame in some way. Anyhow, after that I found Jenny's book, *Angel Whispers*, and I haven't looked back since. Three months ago I met a great guy called James, and I really think we have a chance together. I actually want to settle down!

PAST-LIFE ISSUES

My book *Soul Angels* goes into this subject fully, but there's no doubt that past-life issues, traumas and hang-ups can prove to be a stumbling block when it comes to our spiritual path, as Jennie's story above demonstrates. Our soul angels are there to help us out with this, and once they've nudged us into taking the right action to solve past-life carry-overs, it certainly clears the way for other sorts of angel encounters. It was only once I'd resolved my past-life issues that I developed a deep angelic connection. It was only a couple of months afterwards that I had my first and probably most dramatic angel encounter. I'd like to also share Elise's story with you here. It's a very dramatic example both of how a soul angel operates, and the effect it can have on further angelic communication.

My story begins with a dream at four years old. My mother would put me to bed in my large, pale blue bedroom, and as I lay curled up on my side looking at a painting on the wall, I imagined all the creatures from the picture going about their daily business. There were foxes, rabbits, squirrels, badgers, mice, birds, a woodland scene with all the characters dressed up and going shopping, riding bicycles, cleaning windows and living like little people in their tiny village made of trees. Then I would look up at a hole in the ceiling where a pipe ran into the loft and, in my imagination, a fox would come running down the pipe.

At this point I began to hear the footsteps and my heart would beat with fear. 'Don't make me go, Mummy, please don't make me go with him. The Sandman's coming, Mummy, please don't make me go,' I'd plead. But she told me that I had to. There was no choice in the matter. I'd hear the boots, black boots ... thump, thump, thump and, terrified, I'd be put in a cart and taken away. Then I was in some kind of bath house where all was a kind of sepia colour. There were many women in the same room and none of us had clothes on. I was about eight years old and aware that my auntie and a sister were also there. Then I would wake up, still terrified.

The dream was recurrent for a long time until eventually I stopped dreaming about the Sandman, the cart and all the naked women in the bath house. The memory of it all, however, stayed with me for life.

I was born in 1957, the middle daughter of three female siblings to Jewish parents, neither of whom had any direct experience of the Holocaust. My mother recalls her own mother taking in a Jewish refugee in Manchester during the Second World War, and eventually learning about the horrors of the Holocaust through the media. My father joined the Royal Air Force and spent time as a radio engineer in Egypt and the Middle East, but had no connection with what was going on in wartime Europe. As children, we were overprotected to the point of being smothered and shielded from anything to do with the attempt to obliterate an entire race, my own race. At four years old, I knew nothing about the Holocaust, and yet it seemed as though my dream was triggered by an inexplicable memory of something terrifying and horrific.

A shy and nervous child, school terrified me. Uniforms made me very uncomfortable. The showers at school during adolescence were an experience I had to avoid at all costs, as the mere thought of having to take off my clothes in front of others scared me, as some may state, 'to death'. Desperately unhappy in a rigidly controlled academic institution, I was asked to leave my grammar school at 14 due to my work not being up to standard. The reason was the fact that the school environment, to me, felt like some kind of prison camp, the teachers like Gestapo officers, and I was bullied and called a 'fat Jew girl'. I recall an incident at the age of 13 when my mother took me to have my hair cut. The hairdresser cut it too short for my liking and I screamed with horror, demanding my mother should buy me a wig to cover up the short hair. I wore the wig until my hair had grown back to what I considered to be an acceptable length. On another occasion, at the dentist, I began to scream with terror as he pulled a tooth, my reaction prompted by a vision of some other world or lifetime.

By the time I reached 15, as a misfit and a victim, I had taken my first overdose. The second followed in my early twenties during my first marriage. My career was unstable until my second marriage, motherhood and an opportunity to enter an open-ended period of psychotherapy. When my son started school, I resumed a Counselling

Diploma which I had started years previously but had been unable to continue due to financial circumstances.

Five years' intensive study, following years of spiritual searching, inner exploration and working with alternative therapists looking at the possibility of past lives led to a Master's degree in Psychotherapy and Healing at the age of 52. A big achievement for someone who had left school with two 'O' levels! My dissertation was based upon my own spiritual journey and the research which I had undertaken into past-life therapy and the question of the transmission of memory for second- and third-generation Holocaust survivors.

As part of my research I undertook various forms of regression therapy. In every regression I found myself, after being captured by the Nazis, standing in a line of naked women. There were piles of suitcases on the ground, reading glasses, hair from where heads had been shaved, and clothes. Screams could be heard where teeth were being pulled out. And then the showers. But they weren't showers at all and I screamed as the gas was turned on and I knew that I was going to die. But I was only eight years old. I knew nothing of death. Surrounded by terrified women, I was nevertheless completely alone. During one regression session on a weekend workshop with Dr Roger Woolger (author of *Other Lives, Other Selves*), after 're-experiencing' the death and while in trance, I found myself travelling through layers of grey fog until colours changed and became lighter. A short transcript of part of the session follows.

'Suffocating, no breathing ... it's over? [Where are you?] I don't know. [Can you see your body?] It's on the ground, still in the room, I'm not dead yet. My body is huddled on the floor, there are other bodies around ... above ... I don't know what's happened. Where's Mummy? I left my doll ... they all look lost ... it's like it's all grey ... why's it all grey? It's cold, so cold ... I don't understand life is over ... I don't know what happens after people die ... crying ... why did Mummy go? Why did she leave me? Crying ... holding the crying in, can let it out now...

'I can see down ... piles of clothes, piles of glasses [what happens to the body, you're not in it any more]. The smell, burning, big fires ... it's not me, it used to be ... [feel the separation] I stay a long time looking for Mummy ... can't find anyone now ... floating above it ... just cold, still looking for Mummy. It's like we're all lost, we're in a mass of grey hovering over, all confused ... stay there for some time ... confused ... bewildered ... bodies are being thrown into a furnace ... I see my body being thrown in...

'It's getting lighter. The colours change, different colours, still cold, shivering and trembling ... I see what's happening still ... more people going in, and smoke, and screaming ... they're pulling teeth out ... coughing, changing colour, orange, green, pink, gold ... all changing everywhere ... like a tunnel I suppose ... still so cold, so cold...

'There's something at the end of the "tunnel", a gold figure, an angel? Arms outstretched ... I can come, it's OK. Will Mummy be there? He says it's OK. Embraces me, bit warmer ... "I'll take you." He's taking me to Mummy ... crying, crying ... is it all right now? It's not cold any more. An energy ... [ask why she left] ... they took her away, that's why she sent me away, she hoped I'd escape ... she holds me for a long time...'

The most profound part of that session and the most healing (termed in therapeutic language 'healing in the Bardo', the Tibetan Buddhist term for the realm to which we go after we have passed) was meeting the most amazing light being, a golden figure of pure loving energy – what I felt must surely be some kind of angel.

The following year we were travelling in Egypt and spending a week in Aswan. While relaxing by the hotel swimming pool, I noticed an attractive older woman moving her hands around one of the guests who lay with her eyes closed on a sunbed in the shade. She was dressed modestly in the style of a smart Muslim woman, complete with headscarf, although she was a white woman and not Egyptian. Being familiar with many types of spiritual healing, this was nothing new for me but I was intrigued to speak to her and approached her when she had completed the healing process with which she had been working.

Over the course of the next few days I came to know Ingrid Hartmann/Fatima as a friend, healer and profound mystic (married to a younger Egyptian man, she had taken the Muslim faith as her own, hence the traditional dress). I arranged a healing session with her for the following day and we agreed to meet in the hotel lobby. As I went to greet her at the arranged time, she immediately took something from her handbag and said to me, 'A healer friend of mine gave this to me and said that it was yours – it is a picture of the angel Uriel,' and handed me what looked like a photograph. It was identical to the figure that I had seen/met during my regression session – an angel of golden light.

I have seen so many people change their lives and turn things around through listening to their soul angels and addressing past-life issues. Once they've done that, the connection to their guardian angel appears to be almost automatic, as the healing their soul receives sends their vibration skyrocketing. My website has a very comprehensive worldwide list of past-life therapists on it. Unfortunately, although I'm qualified, one needs to be insured to carry out this work, and as I find I have very little time nowadays to do one-to-one sessions, it isn't viable so I have to leave actual regressions to those who do it full time.

GIVING UP

In one of my past lives I gave up totally. My husband of the time had been kidnapped and I believed him to be dead. My resolve and my spirit collapsed and in that time of spiritual weakness I killed myself. It wasn't an answer, because in this lifetime I have to face a similar scenario. My current husband was diagnosed with a possible life-threatening illness. I almost collapsed again. I almost gave up again. Thank goodness, this time I was more connected spiritually and I was able to withstand the stresses, barely, and come through the other side. Suicide is the ultimate in giving up, but people give up in other much less dramatic ways, too. They decide they just aren't worth it, or they haven't got an angel, or even that their angel hates them. They won't listen to advice, especially from someone like me who seems to have the perfect life, compared to theirs anyway. People who have read my book *Souls Don't Lie* know that I haven't had the perfect life at all, and in fact I don't honestly know anyone who has. It's very tough I know to pick yourself up off the bottom of the barrel and drag yourself up out of a pit of depression, because I've been there and done that. The thing to remember if you're in this position is that it's probably not going to happen overnight, although that too is possible, and that baby steps are the only way forward.

I would recommend anyone having this kind of problem to go for past-life regression for a start. At the very least it will help them learn to relax, through being able to understand themselves better, through healing troubling phobias that may be affecting life quality, right up to complete healing and figuring out their path in life. After that they need to generate tiny sparks of happiness wherever possible, and like a well-nurtured seed they will grow and increase exponentially. Life isn't meant to be so tough and it can improve with a connection to angels, which will come with positive energy. If the person is ill, they should accept that this could be past-life generated. Once they've done that and taken appropriate steps to heal it, they must also address the illness itself, because they have to deal with themselves holistically: mind, body and spirit. Just healing one of these aspects of ourselves might not be enough. To this end, at the back of the book where I've listed resources, two of them are health-related. Anyone suffering a serious illness will find help there.

IMPATIENCE

This is where I hold up my hand and plead guilty! I am often impatient in life, wanting everything to happen to my schedule and not heaven's. It's something I came here this time to work on and, thank angels, I'm starting to get there. The thing is that, as our angels see it, they have all of eternity, if necessary, to help us get where we're meant to be and get it all right. As we see it, however, it's hard to see further than our human lifespan at the time. Compared to eternity, this is very short indeed. We must trust that our angels do know best and if we can learn to just 'accept' their help and their timescale, it's surprising how things can actually turn around quicker than if we'd huffed and puffed and stressed. Because, as I'm sure you all know by now, stress equals negative energy.

MOST IMPORTANT FACT

No one else has control over any of the issues
discussed in this chapter. You have control.

CHAPTER 8

Communicating with Angels through Chakras, Labyrinths and Sound Vibration

First of all I'd like to explain what a chakra is. Chakras are your energy centres. They are the 'openings' that allow energy to flow from your body into your aura. It's your chakras that determine the colour of your aura. Different chakras generate different colours, and this is why an aura reader can sometimes tell what issues and which areas of your physical body need attention by reading the colours of your aura. There have traditionally been seven chakras, although some people believe there are now more than that. (More on this later.)

THE SEVEN TRADITIONAL CHAKRAS

THE SEVENTH CHAKRA

Otherwise known as the crown chakra, this relates to what you've learned and how enlightened you have become, which explains its proximity to your brain, where it covers both left- and right-brain function. Its colour is usually a pure bright white, especially when it is emitting angelic energy, but it can also be gold or violet. More gold would indicate some karmic issues needing attention, but also the power and knowledge to deal with this information. Violet would tend more toward a growing psychic ability.

THE SIXTH CHAKRA

Otherwise known as the third eye, this is in the centre of the forehead, just above the eyebrows. This is the 'eye' that is said to be opened to admit psychic visions and previews of the future. Because of this the colour is usually violet. It also deals with situations that have required you to use reasoning and intuition.

THE FIFTH CHAKRA

Otherwise known as the throat chakra, this should normally be blue. However, when I do aura readings, this area can be many different colours and can indicate a need for the person to speak out more – or less. It obviously deals with communication issues, and as this is an area with which many people have trouble, it's a very important chakra to clear when trying to create wellbeing.

THE FOURTH CHAKRA

This is located in the centre of the chest, often also called the heart chakra, so as you can imagine it deals with love and relationship issues. Emotional pain in this area will show up as red, but when the person is balanced it will be pink. The energy this chakra generates is the same energy that is used to bring guides closer to you. Someone well linked to their guides will have a green and pink colour.

THE THIRD CHAKRA

This is situated in the solar plexus, and is the centre of your life-force. Due to this, health issues will often show here, and I find that when I'm doing readings, this is where allergies show up – for instance, white dots indicate a dairy allergy. This is also the centre of your self-confidence and is the place where you'll feel any fear you have. When balanced it should be yellow.

THE SECOND CHAKRA

A couple of inches below your navel, this is called the sacral chakra. When this area is clear and the energy is flowing well, this chakra will be orange. It deals with home and security, and is also the centre for fertility, so if a person is trying for a baby they should strive to have this chakra as free as possible. Having a suitable 'nest' is, of course, essential to the health of this chakra.

THE FIRST CHAKRA

This is low down on the abdomen, level with the bottom of the spinal column. This is the chakra that helps you stay grounded. It is your base. Obviously it's essential to have a firm foundation, and a clear base chakra should be red, the colour of flames for power and energy, and it can also be an earthy red, signifying a strong connection to the planet.

CLEARING YOUR CHAKRAS

Clearing your chakras is a very good start toward creating the right energy for angel connection. Some people find the following the easiest kind of meditation, because they find it easy to visualize things happening in their own actual body, rather than something plucked out of their imagination.

Have a notepad and pen on your lap, or within easy reach.

The most important thing to aim for is simply to relax. Picture each chakra in turn, feeling the corresponding part of your body as you do. Imagine your chakras as anything that you find easy to 'see', such as flowers, spinning circles or butterflies. Before you bring each one to mind, take three deeps breaths, breathing in through your nose and out through your mouth. As you progress through your chakras, picture each one being gently bathed in pure, white light. Imagine the light permeating the flower, the circle or the butterfly, filling it with a glow. As each chakra is cleansed, ask your angel to come near you and to give you a message. If you hear anything at all, in your mind or out loud, pause for a moment and jot it down on the pad. If not, then proceed to the next chakra.

Once you've cleansed each chakra and every one is sparkling clean, ask your angel once more to come close and speak to you. Now that you've cleansed all the chakras, it should be easier. Once you feel you have received all you're going to for this session, travel down each chakra again and close them. You must do this because open chakras invite energy in, rather than sending it out, and you don't want a negative energy sneaking in. To do this, visualize a flower closing into a tight bud. If you've been visualizing a spinning circle, see it spinning tighter and tighter until it's just a dot. If you're using the butterfly image, have the butterfly close its wings flat together. Jot down anything that comes to mind while you're doing this so that later you can see what was given to you.

NEW CHAKRAS

Some people believe that we're developing new chakras that will descend further down our bodies, into our legs and feet. They say that these will ensure that, as our general vibration rises, which it will as more people are taking the trouble to cleanse their own energy systems, we will retain a close connection to the planet.

Other people say that the new generation of indigo and crystal children are born with extra chakras and have 13 chakras in all. The 13th chakra in particular will be strongly associated with angel energy.

I really believe that whatever feels most comfortable to you is, in this case anyway, the best way for you to utilize your chakras to create an angel connection.

LABYRINTHS

Another very effective and very little used way to connect with your angels is through labyrinths. These devices can produce incredible and startling results, and if you're having trouble connecting to angels, they could well be your way forward.

People are often confused and think that labyrinths are the same as mazes. This isn't the case. A maze is meant to be a puzzle. You go in one end and you're meant to find the easiest and quickest way out again, without coming back out the same way. It's usually constructed of hedges, and of course the 'walls' have to be above the eye line otherwise there would be no puzzle. They are for entertainment purposes only. A labyrinth, on the other hand, is a spiritual journey to self-discovery, both literally and figuratively, and they have been around for over 4,000 years. You go in one end, find your way to the centre, and then retreat back the same way, retracing your steps. In a labyrinth, the entrance is also the exit. Labyrinths can be made of stones, hedges, even insulating tape stuck to a pavement. It doesn't matter if you can see all the way to the centre. The idea is that you follow the path to the middle, following the twists and turns, ending up symbolically at *your* centre. The journey will encourage switches from your right brain to your left brain and back. In this way it can greatly enhance your consciousness. When you reach the centre, with the proper state of mind you can choose what to confront. Your fears or your past can be recognized at the centre and accepted, and then you can choose to leave them behind when you embark on your journey back to the world. Or you can ask that your angel be there to meet you at the centre. In this sacred space you'll be cut off from the world and all its distractions. If you walk a labyrinth in the right state of mind, you'll forget that the 'walls' are only six inches high if they're marked out with rocks, or imperceptibly high if made from masking tape.

You can walk into another dimension in a labyrinth, and once you've tried it you'll likely become hooked. Once you reach the centre, you can just wait and 'expect' your angel's presence to make itself felt. Some people find this is the only way to connect with their angels and, as I've said, you can construct one yourself using one of the many drawings that are available. However, using a labyrinth that already exists, and has existed for centuries, can add a spiritual dimension to your journey. Knowing that thousands of people have walked the route before you can be very powerful. Because of this I've added (in the Resources section) a very useful labyrinth locator website address which will help you find your nearest labyrinth.

SOUND VIBRATION

> *Do you know that our soul is*
> *composed of harmony?*
>
> – **Leonardo da Vinci**

Every living thing and every energized thing vibrates. Pythagoras said,

Each celestial body, in fact each and every atom, produces a particular sound on account of its movement, its rhythm or vibration. All these sounds and vibrations form a universal harmony in which each element, while having its own function and character, contributes to the whole.

The key to being in tune with these vibrations, whether it be with crystals or angels, can lie with discovering what their vibration is and endeavouring to match it somehow. With crystals, just hold one in your hand and use your intuition to 'feel' the answer. With angels you can ask, once you have a connection. Sometimes in both cases you'll get a certain note, which can be recreated by the use of a particular crystal singing bowl or a musical instrument. Sometimes it can be something like the song of a robin, or the sound of waves crashing on a rocky shore. All is sound.

This is also why music is so important to humans. No human child grows up, even in the poorest places, without at some point revelling in the power of sound. It gets inside you and makes you feel whatever the rhythm within it wants you to feel. Sound vibration and music are very powerful tools indeed.

Pythagoras also said, 'The highest goal of music is to connect one's soul to their Divine Nature, not entertainment.' What do you hear when you play music? Do you just hear a clever and pleasing combination of notes, or something infinitely deeper? The resonant power of sound can actually change the rate of vibration in the whole molecular structure. My first experience of this was with crystal singing bowls. I'd heard of and seen Tibetan bowls, which are metal, but these were something new. The bowls are a by-product of Silicon Valley. They are used in the 'growing' of silicon chips. This is because quartz crystals, from which they are made, resonate very uniformly, and this is also why the crystals are used in machines that require very accurate calibration. The bowls have silicon placed in their centre and are vibrated. This causes the silicon to form up into pillars, which are then thinly sliced into chips.

The most dramatic use of these bowls is to place one on a person's abdomen while they lie down. When the bowl is vibrated in this position, the resonance goes deep into the body, and the result is quite amazing. Your whole body feels realigned and cleansed by this procedure. This experience of mine was coupled with another that brought home to me the power of sound. We were attending a meditation initiated by crystal bowl singing. The room was darkened and the sounds soon induced a kind of trance. This was broken by a strange sound that seemed to be coming from the woman playing the bowls. The hairs on the back of my neck stood up, and talking afterwards with the other participants confirmed that they all felt the same as I did. I had never heard anything like that growling sound, and I wondered if some wildcat had snuck into the room, or indeed whether the bowl played had transformed into something quite unworldly.

It transpired that she was actually performing something called 'over-toning'. If you've never heard it, be warned: it can be frightening and immensely, instinctually worrying. It's rumoured that churches banned this form of sound at one point, and it certainly has a quality that could be misconstrued as evil, if you weren't warned about it. However, over-toning is actually an advanced form of vocal harmonics. It's the process of creating two or more notes at the same time, as used by Tibetan monks and Mongolian shamans.

It's said that many forms of vocal harmonics are capable of changing the rhythms of our heartbeats and respiration as well as our brainwaves. This is possible because the brain itself is a device created to send and receive information, and as these sounds can affect and change the vibration patterns of different parts of the brain, they can actually retune it.

If you doubt that sound can have such a dramatic effect, then consider the sounds of dolphins. It's scientific fact that these incredible mammals can actually totally change the behaviour of autistic children and those suffering from Down's Syndrome and other neurological and motor diseases. While the very presence of these animals can account for some changes, it can only be the sounds that make possible the claims that the physical structure of fluids and tissues in the children's bodies actually changes, too, facilitating healing.

Another sacred connotation of sound is in the use of chanting. Mantras are phrases, single words or syllables repeated continuously. It is really another way of focusing the mind away from conscious thoughts, and will help raise your spiritual vibration and enable communication with the higher realms. Examples vary from the well-known 'Om' chant through to more complex and multi-syllable chants, depending on the reason for the chanting and which God or deity is being approached.

But even the simple and non-religious pastime of humming is known to induce calm and soothe the mind. This must confirm that sound does indeed affect the brain.

There are many instruments that are evocative, and none more so that the Aboriginal didgeridoo. Many consider that it is probably the world's oldest musical instrument; its origins are believed to lie in the distant past of 40,000 years ago, therefore pre-dating even the drum. They are made from eucalyptus branches that have already been hollowed out by termites. The Aborigines have a legend which explains the creation of the stars to them. They say that their God, Wurrawurra, first made a tree and then some termites to eat out the centre of a branch. Then he came back, broke off the branch and blew into it. The termites flew out of it on his mighty breath and whirled up into the heavens to form the stars.

Of all the musical instruments, the didgeridoo is also probably one of the most mesmerizing. A group of skilled players can totally entrance listeners. This is because its tones and overtones are deep and vibrational. They were certainly used by Aborigines to induce 'dream-time', in which they would experience visions. Since the birth of healing sounds in the New Age arena, didgeridoos have enjoyed a resurgence. This has also meant that the art of playing them, rather than dying out, has become more widespread.

When it comes to angels, we know their vibration is much higher than ours, and one way to try and alter our own brainwaves to match theirs is with a tool that can lift our vibration by using any of the above instruments. If you feel this might be a way forward for you, then I can recommend being taught by someone like Diane Egby of Bournemouth (see the Resources chapter), who is an authority on the science of sound as well as its spiritual and mystical qualities.

MOST IMPORTANT FACT

Ancient cultures held a lot of knowledge that's lost today. Reclaim this wisdom by learning how to create your own specially tailored vibrational healing.

CHAPTER 9

Communicating through Art and Creativity

Working creatively with paints or pens, clay or other sculptural material can open your subconscious and is a very useful device if you find meditation difficult and deep relaxation impossible. Writing is another tool which is sometimes underrated. For instance, when I'm working on a book, I find that most of it is given to me. Sometimes I get the next part to be written in the night, sometimes while I'm actually working. Either way, when I'm 'in the zone' – in other words, concentrating on the words – Tony can ask me questions and I'll even answer him in a logical way, but later I'll have no recollection of the conversation at all. I've lost count of the number of cups of tea that have gone cold and unnoticed right by my elbow. This type of mindset/brainwave can be used productively. When I'm in this state my angels can talk to me directly, and yours could talk to you, too. So try any one of these things. Release the creative artist in you – you don't have to be a world-beater at any of them, just so long as you let your energy flow free as your mind focuses on nothing.

Caroline told me the story of how her art grew and affected many other people, and also gave her insight into her own life.

When I was born in 1945 in Takapuna, New Zealand, I would never have imagined that by today I would be married to an English clairvoyant, have discovered my own way of communicating with angels through art and sent spiritual guidance to a condemned murderer on death row!

I started learning art quite by mistake. I had intended to learn macramé, but I went through the wrong door and found myself joining a class learning to paint. Of course by now I know that there is no such thing as a 'wrong' door, and that all doors opened for us are intentional. Three years later my first husband and I moved to Wanganui to set up a regional distribution business. I was fully occupied for some time, living in an old farmhouse, raising pet lambs, children, chickens and pigs, as well as organizing deliveries of stock to local supermarkets and schools.

Art called me back six years later and I studied for a Fine Arts degree. At this time I started to feel that my brush was guided, and my tutors were often surprised by the work I turned out. It was, at times, like someone else was doing it, rather than me.

A few years later my marriage broke up and I went to see my elderly father, who was dying of emphysema and cancer. After he died I was alone in the house, and this was when I started to really feel the influence of spirit in my work.

I had a relative who was having very serious drug problems, and I found myself doing a picture of a shaman for him. I felt this would help to guide him into healing. Now, 15 years later, that picture still watches over him as he enjoys his life as a happy, healthy father of teenage girls.

In 1992 I came to live and work in England. One day a series of little synchronicities led me to a bookshop in Taunton, Somerset. There I met my beloved husband, Lawrence. We were married within months. Lawrence is a skilled psychic who uses numerology and tarot. He is further along his spiritual pathway than I am, and therefore he has been able to guide me and tell me what my pictures meant. With his encouragement I learned to really let go, using my left hand (I am normally right-handed) so that I could be sure that spirit was guiding my hands rather than my own mind. This felt very strange at first, but as time went by I adjusted. I learned to listen to being told what colours to use, and exactly where to put a mark, whether to press hard or softly, and I've even been told to wash my hands at one point to keep the colours vibrant! Sometimes I am instructed to turn the picture round, scribble on it furiously, rub it with my fingers, and have even had to throw water on it! Lawrence's presence seemed to amplify things so that my work became stronger and stronger.

One very strange thing that happened was again due to synchronicity. I was 'led' to a small giftshop in the Forest of Dean when I was out for a drive one day. I got chatting to the woman behind the counter and, after a while, she unexpectedly asked me if I had ever thought of writing to prisoners on death row in the USA. She explained that they are locked up and chained 22 out of 24 hours, not allowed radio, books or newspapers, and only a little contact with their families, most of whom don't want to know them anyway. The woman belonged to a worldwide organization that organized letter-writing to that sort of prisoner. If I decided to do it I would have to commit to writing 22 letters a month for 18 months, up until their executions were carried out.

I couldn't commit to all those letters as I had enough on my plate writing home to New Zealand every week. I had showed the woman one of my paintings, and she asked if she could have it for her father-in-law, who was in the early stages of Alzheimer's. She told me later that he cried when he saw it, and used to spend hours at a time just looking at it. This gave her an idea, and she asked me if I would do a painting for each of the death-row prisoners. She was honest, though, saying that she didn't think there was much chance of them getting through. She also warned me that I would get no acknowledgement or feedback.

Over the next week I got myself in a bit of a state as, just at the same time, Fred West's horrific crimes were being revealed and I wondered about the wisdom of putting my heart and soul into paintings that were going to the likes of him! I thought I'd be helping someone who didn't deserve it. After much soul-searching I came to realize that it wasn't up to me to be judge and jury, as they had already been condemned to die. I've always hated being confined or closed into small places and from that point of view I felt for them. I also felt that the weird circumstances of my meeting this woman, and her asking me out of the blue, meant that it was all meant to be, so I decided to go ahead.

For two weeks I worked on my 22 pictures, which had to be kept small by request. I'd never done landscapes before, but I had often admired the country mornings and sunsets, so that was what I painted. I lit candles and prayed to be guided to create images that would help them, and some came out unbelievably beautiful. There were sweeping hills and valleys, lit by gentle light that glowed in the early morning or evening. I actually did 23 pictures, one of which I sent my mother for a surprise.

Finally I took the 22 paintings back to the woman in the shop, and when she laid them out on her floor, she cried. They seemed to radiate peace, hope, light and comfort. Two months later I contacted her, and to my amazement she told me that against all odds the pictures had got through. The prisoners were allowed to pin them up on the walls. She was also able to tell me that each prisoner had received one. She said that, most amazingly, one man in particular said that he had been so terrified of dying before he got my painting, but that somehow he now knew that there was literally light at the end of his tunnel. He was able to go to his death and meet his Maker with hope.

I have also done paintings for sick people, for instance a seven-year-old boy who was having open-heart surgery.

'Look Mum,' he said, 'There is the world, and I am going to go round it one day.' He made a full recovery. It never fails to amaze me that people all see something unique for themselves in each painting. I have done pictures that just look like a mess to me, but the person it is for will tell me that they can see their past and a better future in it.

These days when Lawrence does an evening of tarot and numerology, I go with him, and I tune in to the people in the audience and ask my guides for an appropriate picture for each person. The results are an assortment of guides, angels, passed members of people's families or just a representation of where a person is at that moment in time. Lawrence is nationally known as a numerologist and tarot reader and he also teaches people his craft in workshops. Lawrence's philosophy is to give honest guidance and upliftment from the cards in a lovely relaxed and friendly manner. He feels very strongly that no one should ever leave a clairvoyant reading feeling down and says that, if you do, then it wasn't a good clairvoyant. Clear, loving and sympathetic guidance is the order of the day. Lawrence is one of life's genuine gentlemen and has 30 years' experience of working with the cards – no wonder I fell in love with him at first sight!

Two weeks before Lawrence and I were married, I did what looked like a surreal scribble in sea-green. Nothing realistic was discernable in the painting. But we really liked it, so much so that we had it framed. Two weeks before our first wedding anniversary I suddenly realized that it had changed. Looking at the changes closely we could clearly make out a 1920s couple standing there. He is wearing a flat cap and waistcoat, and she has a wedding dress and long veil. Lawrence and I always felt we had known each other before, and we believe that the painting now shows us on a previous wedding day in a former life in the 1920s.

ART IN PHOTOGRAPHY

Challenge yourself to be creative in the photos you take. Today with digital photography you can snap away at little cost. Try bringing different areas into focus. Look at light and shadow as well as just colour. Capture a sunrise or a sunset to uplift you and everyone who looks at it. Use your camera to create permanent memories you can revisit at any time. Experiment with composition, making different things the centre of attention. See if you can create photography that affects other people's energy when they look at it.

SINGING

Opening the vocal cords and getting emotionally involved in a song can also change your energy. If you can become part of a group or choir, all the better. Being part of a team can enhance all areas of your life as well as providing you with a support network when you need it, and all these things create a positive aura around you.

NUMBERS

The science of numbers can be brought into the world of angels through numerology. This translation of letters and dates into numerological symbols is a very old practice. There are many good books out there that will help you use this tool to connect with your higher self in a way that should appeal to the more logical minds among you. There's a symmetry to it that doesn't require any 'mumbo-jumbo'. It's all very easy to believe because it has definite structure, and can be a great stepping stone into using your intuition just a little, without, if you're a doubter, feeling silly.

As with everything I suggest, always state your intent to your angels first. If you make sure they're 'on board' in every spiritual endeavour, you'll never get tangled up in anything dark. Your intent is always 'for the highest good'. To demonstrate the power of numerology, let me share this letter from my column in Australia's *Take 5* magazine. A mum called Deanna Browne recently sent me a photo (ultrasound image) of her unborn little girl with this letter.

Dear Jenny

This ultrasound photo of my baby girl was taken eight weeks ago and I was wondering. Near her mouth you can see a bubble of fluid that she's blowing out of her mouth, and if you look closely you can see a number actually in the fluid, the number six. Is it a sign of some sort? Her name will be Shayla Grace Mills, and she is due on 5 August. Can you see how much she will weigh at all, as I have gestational diabetes and am hoping that she won't be too small?

Here is my answer to her:

In numerology your baby's name adds up to the number 3. If we add this to her expected birth date we can see what she's trying to tell you. She will be born a day early, so be prepared! I know this because if you add 4 (rather than the predicted 5 August) to 8, that equals 12, which added together equals 3, which added to her name value gives 6. Also, it's confirmed, because if you add the whole date together as $4 + 8 + 2 + 0 + 1 + 0$, that makes 15, and $1 + 5$ equals 6 again! What will she weigh? That's easy! Six pounds!

This is a real long-shot to have happen randomly, because every letter has a different value in numerology.

Today, when I was at Blackberry Camp, which is described in the next chapter, I was given an insight (as is often the case when I'm writing books) to do with this chapter on creative connections. It was to do with the word 'imagine'. Imagination has always, to me, been the same as 'meditation'. When children play in an imaginary world, when we try to visualize an imaginary future we hope to manifest, we are all meditating. Sometimes when we have something wonderful happen, like a vision or an angelic message comes through, sceptical people might say it was just 'imagination'. But what is imagination if not the tuning in to our higher selves? And who is to say that what we get is not only imagination, but also magical, mystical and real? So, back to today. The word 'imagine' can be used as a tool, to reassure and to focus. Say it this way – IMAGE IN, for this is its true meaning. What we see as an 'image' should be welcomed 'in'. There is an old saying: 'If you can IMAGE IN it, then you can do it,' and it is very true, as was confirmed to me today.

MOST IMPORTANT FACT

Meditation is not as difficult as people think. All you
have to do is become 'absorbed' in something and
your mind will casually slip into a meditative state.
There are more tips on ways to do this in
the next chapter.

CHAPTER 10

Unusual Ways to Receive an Angel Message

Think of it this way: meditation, or in other words raising your vibration, is just switching off the everyday world and its everyday problems and concerns. If it doesn't suit you, you don't have to lie in a darkened room. For some people when they do this, the moment they shut their eyes to try and shut off the world, the very opposite happens and the world comes rushing in instead. For them, more unusual ways have to be found. There are many ways to try and get a sign from your angel that can be quite fun. As I've shown, angels do like a bit of fun sometimes, so if you give your angel an opportunity to respond in a synchronistic way, they'll often take it.

TREE HUGGING

I know many people who like to hug trees. They get comfort from it, and some go as far as being able to feel the sap (energy) rising in the tree, especially if they do it in the spring, when every living thing is reaching out. But it can go a lot further than that. Trees, like angels (although on a much simpler scale) are conduits to the universe. It's much easier to connect with those lofty higher dimensions, where the angels live, if you have a friendly tree to help you.

The first thing to do is to select your tree. For the best results it should be mature and healthy, and if possible on a very ancient site that has its own energy, such as an iron-age hill fort or in a very old forest. Place your hands on the tree, as if you were hugging it, and make sure the length of your body and one side of your face are in contact with the tree. Then just relax, let go and feel for energy through your skin. After a while, with patience, you'll start to get a sense of the energy running up the centre of the tree like a pulsing river. This is the sap rising. Wait a while and you'll start to feel as if your body is being absorbed into the tree – you'll just sink into darkness, full of swirling energy, and your spirit will start to rise up with the sap. Relax a while, just breathe, and soon you'll find universal energy coming down to meet you as you rise toward it. Listen in your mind for messages, or if you need healing, reach up toward your angels and ask. You'll feel your being start to glow and buzz, and healing will start. Take as much as you can until you literally feel full from your toes to the top of your head.

Today I visited a new place I'd never been before. It's near where we live on the edge of Somerset, but in Devon, just over the border. It's an iron-age hill fort known as Blackberry Camp, or Blackberry Castle. A good friend of mine, Rosemarie Davies, who knew I'd appreciate it, told me about it, saying it was magical. She was right. When I first walked into the circle of mature beech trees I was hit right away by their majesty, but also by the scent of the masses and masses of bluebells that cast a swirling blue sea throughout the circle of the fort banks. Tears came to my eyes as I took in the indigo splendour of the wild flowers. Bluebells have a very special meaning for me from a past-life incident, and they always touch me, and this field of blue was the best I have ever seen. It has to be like these were, native bluebells, smaller and brighter than their cultivated cousins. The place had no official ancient name, as of course there were no records back then, but that was to change, for me anyway. I chose a tree. It wasn't easy, surrounded as I was by incredibly beautiful, huge beech trees, their fresh spring leaves acid green against the blue sky. But eventually I was able to make a choice. Once I did and was connected with my chosen tree, it told me, 'This place is Holy Heart.' How beautiful. Tree after tree confirmed this name, and I felt very privileged to know what the people who'd lived in the settlement had once called their home. I was also told it was a safe place, and it truly was one of the most peaceful and energizing areas I have ever visited.

Healers in days of old used to have their patients stand naked under an oak tree in the rain. They believed that the rainwater collected energy from the tree as it drained down through the leaves. Today we have flower remedies and essences, which are pretty much the same thing when you think of it.

MESSAGE IN A BOTTLE

We've all heard the stories about people stuck on a desert island and sending off a message in a bottle in the hopes of rescue. Or people who use the same method to try and find a friend or even partner. You can also do this with your angel.

Make a little cosmic shopping list of things you'd love in your life, starting with small aspirations and getting bigger as you go down the list. Put it into a bottle (glass, not plastic, please – plastic is killing our oceans) and set it off on an outgoing tide. If the things on your list start to happen, then you'll know your angel is listening and willing to get involved. Or put a little note in a bottle with your e-mail address. Just say something like, 'If an angel gets this message, please could they get in touch.' You could meet someone this way who is destined to change your life in some way, or be a guide on your path. (Never put your phone number or address on the note, for obvious reasons.)

TREE OF PRAYER

If possible it would be very good to actually plant a special tree in your garden. Intent is all to angels and the universe, so if the tree is special you'll be halfway to your goal. The willow tree is a good one for this (but not if you have a small garden – if you have, make sure it's the dwarf variety). Ash is the tree that represents connection, but is a bit messy for small gardens. A flowering cherry tree will fit most gardens, and as well as being beautiful, it represents new awakenings, so it's just about perfect for this.

When the tree is big enough, write messages to your angels on small pieces of paper and peg them (using clothes pegs) onto the branches. The messages should take the form of requests, and as each one is granted by your angel, it should be removed from the tree and burned in a candle flame. Of course you can use an established tree and do the same. It might take a little longer to work, but of course the tree will be bigger to start with so it won't make a lot of difference in the long run.

If you haven't got a garden, don't despair, you can still do this! Go to the nearest public woodland and choose a tree, the more secluded the better. Just go for whichever one you're drawn to, and hang discreet messages on your chosen tree. You might be expecting that people will remove your messages or treat them with disrespect, but in my experience that has never happened.

Hanging messages on tree branches goes back to pagan times and pagan rituals, and really, though they might not admit it, people are generally more at peace with and more connected to their pagan roots than they might realize. Pagan rituals do seem to engender respect in the general population.

Once you have a tree, be it in your garden or elsewhere, try and collect some rainwater from its leaves whenever you can. This pure, tree-energized water can be very healing. You shouldn't drink it, just wash in it.

DIARY

Keep an angel diary. Make a note of any dreams you can recall, or visions during meditations. It's very important to do this, because angels don't have memory problems like we do, and you'll sometimes get so much information that you just can't remember it all. Or your angel, mindful of your limitations, might give you information in segments, and by keeping a dairy you'll keep a record of them all until you can piece them all together. Keep a record of anything your angel does for you, and any little signs you get.

Use your diary to tell your angel about anything that has upset you or made you unhappy. Most likely your angel will show you something amusing the next day to cheer you up. Most important of all, when you're looking for messages and signs, ask your angel whichever questions you need answering in your 'angel diary'. Once you've done this, keep your eyes and ears open the next day to receive your answer. As the next section shows, those answers can come in all manner of ways!

PHOTOGRAPHY

Orbs in photos have become very common nowadays. I think this is in part due to the fact that many more people are taking snaps because it's so easy with digital cameras. Some photos are judged to contain something supernatural, while others are said to just have somehow captured particles of dust or water droplets. Some lights captured are said to be inexplicable, while others are said to be just the effects of the sun or flashes. I have seen many hundreds of both types. My thinking is that sometimes it doesn't matter what caused the anomalies. If you've been looking for an answer and you get one – well, angels work in mysterious ways, just like God! An answer is an answer, even if its method appears mundane.

I was recently sent one photo from a woman in Australia of her parents' old home in England while she was on holiday there. It isn't an orb and it isn't a light. It's a bright, white, smoky shape hovering over the house and is very clearly the perfect shape of an angel. It gave her the ultimate message from her parents: that they are still around, and visit the house, where the woman's brother now lives.

Sometimes passed-over loved ones don't even try to manifest themselves because, to be honest, quite often they would scare the very people they're trying to comfort! So sometimes, instead, they ask their angels to manifest, and that's what I believe happened this time. If you'd like to see this amazing photo, I will be posting it on my website soon, along with some other remarkable pictures that have been sent to me.

GARDENING

Yes, having your hands in the soil and your feet on the ground is a brilliant way to meditate and raise your vibration, almost unawares. Your double connection to the planet and to Nature is very helpful when trying to connect with your angels. Growing things, putting your energy into them and theirs into you can only be beneficial. As you work, take note of any of the world's little wonders that are around you. For instance, did you know that scientists are investigating whether plants can actually count, both warm days and the amount of leaves they have? (See Resources.) Notice any beautifully coloured butterflies, any bejewelled and iridescent beetles. See the ants – think about how all these things work together to form the ecosystems that are your garden. Every time you admire your garden, or the creatures in it, you're helping positivity take hold in your mind, and if you grow some organic vegetables you'll be helping the wildlife and the planet at the same time.

KINDNESS

We've all heard the phrase 'random acts of kindness', and it doesn't take much imagination to make the leap that being kind, especially when there's no real reason to be, perhaps to total strangers, is going to tip the balance for both you and the planet in general toward positivity. Try and do something nice for someone every day without feeling like it's something you *have* to do. Your angels will appreciate it. I'm a great believer also in the 'pay it forward' culture. What this means is that if someone does something nice for you, and doesn't want any payment, then you 'pay it forward' by doing the same, unasked, for someone else, even a random stranger. If they ask what they can do in return, you should say, 'Just pay it forward.'

TELEKINESIS

In this modality you try to tune in to your angels and ask them to help you to move objects without touching them. If you succeed then you'll know that you've also succeeded in raising your vibration enough to reach them.

The best way is to start with a lightweight object, but because of this you must make sure you do it in a draught-proof area and that you don't accidentally affect the object with air movement. A feather, a ball of paper or a straw are quite good examples of easy-to-move objects.

Place the object to be moved in front of you on top of an upturned glass. Some people find that if they hold a crystal in each hand it helps their concentration and prevents static electricity building up. The crystals will also dissipate any positive ions that might be in the room from electrical devices.

The brainwave frequency required to use telekinesis is the same as that which you attain in deep meditation. The idea is not to concentrate on willing the object to move but to 'allow' it to move, by inviting your angels to move it for you and by putting your mind into the correct brainwave frequency and gently channelling the positive energy created toward the object.

Successful practitioners say that eventually you become as one with the object and that even if your eyes are closed, you will feel it move when it finally does.

If you do manage to move something, try and capture the feeling it gave you, because if you can it will be a great help to you the next time you try.

SIGNS OF ANGELIC PRESENCE

I'm lucky enough to be sent many tales of angel encounters and the many and varied ways people get signs of their presence. Here are a few of them.

My favourite way of interacting with the angels when I'm with family and friends is by signs – physical signs such as feathers, clouds and sometimes, on odd occasions, vehicles. One cloud experience I had with the Archangel Gabriel was when I was in the car coming home from college and on the way to the supermarket. I asked one of the angels for a sign of their presence, and when me and my mum parked at the supermarket, I had a feeling to look up – and guess what I saw? I saw a huge cloud in the shape of Gabriel holding his horn.

My most favourite feather experience was with the Archangel Michael, but it had a funny twist to it. I was with my grandparents on a busy day in Sheffield and, because I'm sensitive to emotions and energies, I felt sick and had a headache. I asked for a feather from Michael, but I accidently forgot to be specific about how I wanted this sign. My granddad was sitting down on a bench and behind him was a huge advertisement, and there on the advertisement was a hand holding a giant and pure white feather.

On very rare occasions the angels have shown me signs using the radio. This happened one day when I had a doctor's appointment. I wasn't feel that great and my mum booked me an appointment, and in the waiting room they had a small radio in the corner. Usually I show no interest in it but I listened for some reason and before the doctor called me, a subject came up on this talk show – and guess what the topic was? You guessed it: it was about Archangels.

– Emma

I was on a train going to Manchester once, and I asked, 'Michael can you show me a sign?' and the train went past a warehouse with a huge sign on the side reading ... yup, you guessed it, it said SIGN in big black letters. I then was looking through the Yellow Pages and I said, 'Michael I need a job, please give me a sign what to do.' I flicked the page open right on 'sign makers'. He is so funny, I love having a joke with him.

– *Gemma*

I was feeling quite sad one day, as a good friend and I had fallen out. I wanted to see her, I wanted to talk to her, but you know how it is, you're afraid of rejection. So I sat among the daisies on my back lawn and gazed at the sky for inspiration. I found myself watching the clouds and becoming fascinated with how white and fluffy and sort of 3D they were, floating up there like ships. Then I started noticing that one of them was shaped like a hippo. I smiled at it. I felt better. Then I saw one like a crocodile. Then a giraffe. Then a wolf. When finally one just like an angel with wings appeared, I knew I was getting an angel message. I lived only about five miles from Bristol Zoo, so I thought, why not? I got in the car and went there. I went to the wolf enclosure, and there was Clara, my friend, just sitting watching the wolves. Needless to say, our quarrel was forgotten, and when I told her about how the clouds had led me there, we both laughed and shared a hug.

– Geraldine

When I was around seven years old I saw something I've never really been able to explain. It was early one spring morning at about 6 a.m. and I got out of bed and sat on the window seat looking out of my bedroom window. The sky was a pure blue with no clouds at all. I could see the area of grass out the front of the house and I suddenly noticed something light flitting around out there. It was bright and round and about the size of a walnut. It glowed round the edges and had a lemony halo around it. It seemed to be moving in a deliberate way, and everywhere it passed it left a circle in the grass, which looked at if it were made of frost, although it was much too warm for that. The creature really did look intelligent. It moved with a real sense of purpose. My first thought was that the light was a fairy, and I was full of childish wonder. Apart from that I just accepted it, like it was my secret, and special, but nothing to get too excited about. I watched it for some while before my mum called me, and in an instant I forgot all about it and ran to get my breakfast. Nowadays, though, I do remember it and wonder what it could have been. I wonder if perhaps it was an angel come to help me and

give me strength. I needed it, because the next few years
were very traumatic for me, as I lost my mum and then,
two years later, my dad. I think perhaps that angel, if it
was an angel, wanted me to know I would never really be
alone, and showed itself in the form of what I would per-
ceive as a fairy, so that I'd accept it without a fuss. What I
do know is that it was definitely real.

– Mary

This world is littered with conduits to the realms of angels.
It's just that we often don't recognize them for what they
are. There are those more obvious ones that people with
any ounce of spirituality recognize, such as rainbows, and
then there are the more apparently subtle ones that science
itself needs to understand soon if we are to continue living off this world. The sun and the moon and the oceans
in particular were put here to help us learn to utilize the
planet without destroying the wonderful habitat we have.
They are everything we need. Just as trees depend on the
energy from the sun, so should we. More research must be
done into solar energy, making it more efficient, cheaper
to install and quicker to sustain the people who use it. The
moon provides us with sustainable and carbon-neutral
energy in the form of the tides, which are regular and
relentless, and mostly wasted. The oceans are the beating

heart of planet Earth, and as such they give us the means to propel our 'infernal' engines, using bacterial biofuel from algae. No form of seaweed is poisonous to us, because we came from the sea. It gives us salt, food and energy, if we only had the sense to use it. As we approach a crisis point with this planet, we need angels to light our way and show us what to do to survive in harmony with Nature instead of constantly fighting it.

MOST IMPORTANT FACT

We must learn to live in harmony with the planet, for
in this way we will also live in harmony
with the angels.

Afterword

The main message of this book is that in general you need to cultivate the right energy – that is, positive energy – in order to connect with angels and have your needs fulfilled. I gave you a list of negative emotional states to avoid in order for you to cultivate positive energy. Sometimes, though, it's not easy to recognize your own emotional state. We humans are very good at self-denial, and when asked if we're 'all right', we tend to get defensive and say, 'Yes, I'm fine,' without even really thinking about it. We even tell ourselves that we're fine when we're not, as if saying it will make it so. Also, emotions are constantly shifting as circumstances and thought patterns change and evolve. And it's very easy to react on emotions we never even realize we are experiencing, and in doing so we might upset someone else's emotional stability. The answer is to question yourself constantly: 'What am I feeling right now? Why am I feeling that way? If I react this way or say that, what effect am I trying to achieve, and will it work?'

Quite often we argue with someone, never pausing to understand their dynamics. Most people who get into arguments are intransigent, and trying to bend them to your way of thinking is a waste of energy and can bring you into negativity when otherwise you would have been fine. So, before you enter into a quarrel, ask yourself, 'What do I hope to achieve by this? Is it worth it? Will I ever change this person's mind?' By doing this you'll bring yourself back into balance. After you do this for a while, your natural scales of emotion will start to kick in automatically.

If it helps, visualize an amusing alarm system that will go off whenever negative emotions start to sneak into your thoughts. I find that seeing a little swarm of mini-police swooping down on my negativity works quite well!

If you're expecting a visitor or a phone call from someone who always leaves you feeling negative, question whether you really want this person in your life. If you do, then prepare for their visit by putting a mirror shield around your emotions (see page 28) and then just sit back, relax and enjoy your secret – that no matter how much they try, they won't be able to bring you down. It's a very pleasant sensation if you can achieve it.

HURRY LESS

Try to cultivate a way of being where you always pause before you act or reply. Don't be in too much of a hurry to respond. Consider what results your words or actions will have on the situation, what the response from anyone else is likely to be and, most importantly, what reaction your emotional state is going to have on *you*.

If you do experience a negative emotion, don't panic, just accept it for a moment, then step back, breathe deeply and try to gently but firmly take your mind to another more positive, happy place. Deliberately develop this imaginary positive place in your mind. It can be anywhere you enjoy being, doing anything that fills you with joy. Make it very real by visualizing every tiny detail. Think of this place at least once a day, whether you need to retreat there or not, because this will keep it alive and strong, ready for when you do need it.

When you feel you have a tentative connection with an angel, ask for proof of the connection by requesting something small to start with, like a meaningful street sign or billboard, or by them causing a song to be played on the radio just as you were thinking of it. Baby steps equal angel steps.

Just remember that you only have to make this huge effort once, because once you have a real connection with your angels, so long as you don't tear it away, you'll always have it and every 'next time' you want to connect will be easier than the last.

ANGEL NAMES

Once you have a connection, ask your angels their names. It helps a lot to be able to use their names when you're calling on them. Of course angels don't need names, as they 'see' and recognize each other and souls by their energy, not by name, but it does help us humans if we have something to call them by. There are many ways to do this. You can just shut your eyes and see what comes to you naturally. You can bring up an internet page of angel names and stick a virtual 'pin' in the list. Or you can study names and meanings from whichever culture appeals to you and choose whatever you feel is appropriate. Angels don't mind what you call them.

Don't be too hard on yourself. It takes a lot of practice and determination to make a strong connection with angels and self-doubt or recrimination doesn't help you get there. If at first you don't succeed, then relax, because that *will* help you.

If you've been on a downward spiral for some time, aim low. Accept every tiny second of positive feeling as a triumph. Small triumphs build into huge skyscrapers that can elevate you from the deepest depression.

I'd like to leave the final words to the amazing Nicky Alan, psychic medium and one of the stars of *Angels*, the incredibly popular programme on Sky TV. She is an inspiration to me and a perfect example of someone having trust in the power of angels to help us.

Living in the material world as a spiritual person can sometimes be frustrating and difficult. We can feel angry, stressed and under pressure, and having faith in an invisible force is hard for some people to accept. Having been born with my gift of psychic mediumship, I have never felt alone. However, there have been times when I have felt my life was too difficult and complex and that I wasn't supported spiritually. I now realize that I didn't give the angels permission to involve themselves in my life and that I didn't surrender to their unconditional love and guidance.

I experienced a very traumatic childhood, starting with the tragic passing of my very young dad. Looking back, I took for granted the loveliest voices that would sing to me during my times of fear and loneliness. I would disregard the beautiful people that would visit me enshrouded in a brilliant golden light, all of them with blue shining eyes. Even writing this sends an emotional charge through my body and a tear to my eye. The incredible force of the angels and their unconditional presence in your life is difficult to convey into words if you have never experienced their intervention.

My first visit by an angel was indescribable; he came to me at one of the most desperate times in my life, when I had been retired from the police service after 16 years. I was a lost soul, in complete fear of my future. I saw nothing positive in my life. I felt broken. Very soon after my retirement, the spirit world was in my life with an absolute vengeance. I knew that, whether I wanted it or not, I would be working with the spirit world professionally. Very shortly after I was on my path, working as a full-time medium, I had a powerful visit from an angel.

Please bear in mind, I am a sceptic. I spent 16 years in the police force, a lot of those as a detective. I was a grounded, focused individual who was relentless in seeking truth and justice. Everything, rightly so, had to be presented to a court with irrefutable evidence. So when I tell you about my experiences, they are *real*. They are not figments of my imagination. Believe me, I have tried to see logic, examine coincidence, analyze the events, but I'm sure you will see they speak for themselves.

Because we have obstacles in our lives, because we see the hate in the world, the famine, the war-torn countries, we surmise that there can't be a pure powerful force that is there just to help us. We become a bit cynical. But do you know what? It's there all right!

Shortly after starting my development and full-time mediumship, I did a meditation. As I sat in my energy, I suddenly felt like what I can only describe as the room vibrating. I then had a surge of energy as I saw the most beautiful man I had ever seen. I could smell the sweetest smell as he appeared. He was extremely tall, had the most stunning blue azure eyes, golden blond hair and the most calming, safe energy I had ever felt. He said to me, 'You will now be aware of us whilst you tread your path. Whatever trials lay ahead, call upon us as we will assist you in every way. You are loved from this place and your soul is recognized as belonging with us. Trust us, love us and call us whenever you wish.' As I have already stated, I am a sceptic at the end of the day, but I knew when I came out of this experience that I had been visited by an angel. I was breathing rapidly, heart palpitating and crying tears of, I suppose, joy, relief, amazement, just all different emotions rolled into one.

The energy of the angel felt different from that of loved ones in the spirit world who come to me. It felt stronger and purer. I started to enjoy my newfound relationship with the angels and I knew whenever they had visited or intervened. Their interventions are quick – when you call, they answer – and they are a definitive force so that, when they help you, you feel it so strongly. I have had so many instances where they have helped. Here are a couple of my experiences.

I was due to travel home one night from my ex-partner's mum's house. It was quite a long journey back home. I bent down to get my shoes and heard, 'No!' I felt the force of the voice shiver through my body. I simply walked into the kitchen and said that we were not travelling that night. The following day I heard on the radio that there had been a massive multiple car smash on the motorway. That smash was around the time and on the exact route we would have taken to get home.

The day before I started filming my first series of *Angels* with Gloria Hunniford, I remember lying in the bath terrified about the coming week. I said out loud, 'Am I doing the right thing? Can I represent you to the nation properly? Please help.' No sooner were the words out of my mouth than a feather literally started falling from the ceiling and landed on my left shoulder! And no, I don't have feathered ceilings! All of the feathers that I receive I keep in a dreamcatcher, as I believe they create a hub of positive, divine energy. The most amazing thing for me while filming that series of *Angels* was the fact that all the people who had experienced angel visitation described the same man that I had seen, especially the azure blue eyes. The more I heard their experiences, the more I knew that angels truly are with us.

The angels even, I know, arranged my opportunity to work on television. I remember I was at a time of my life when I was newly single. I was feeling the pressure of having to pay my mortgage alone; I was working very hard and felt exhausted. I was due to go on holiday and really needed to open my horizons up and to reach more people with my work. The day before I went away, I said words to the effect of, 'To my darling angels: I have been working very hard lately and need a rest. I have worked tirelessly representing you and the spirit world to the public. I need to reach more people now; I am ready to open my horizons and need a little help. Please can you help me?' I went away and didn't give it another thought. The day I got home my phone rang. It was the series producer for *Angels.* The production team were looking for someone to carry out angel card readings on their show. He had heard my name being mentioned, had put in a random search and my website came up first. He knew I was the right person for the job, and within two weeks I was filming the first series. Pretty quick work on the angels' part!

Another time I recall was when I was having a very stressful time with a very difficult, angry person who was causing me a lot of harm and pain. The situation had been going on for several months and the police had also been involved. I could not handle the situation anymore and called out to the angels to help. Within ten minutes the phone rang and the friend who'd rung asked if I knew about the Archangel Raguel. I didn't have a clue what she was talking about! I researched the name that she had been given and, unbelievably, Raguel is the Archangel for resolving harmful people and situations. I put his name above my headboard that night, lit a candle and asked Raguel to come and help me. The very next day, after seven months of frustration, I got a telephone call from a colleague who told me that he felt he needed, out of the blue, to contact this person and resolve the issues they had. To this day I have had no further problems.

Last year I was visited by my nan, who has been passed over for a while now. She told me that my mum was going to be poorly but that she would be OK. The following week I got the dreaded call from my mum saying she had been diagnosed with breast cancer. Despite being awfully upset, I knew she would be OK because my nan had said so. I asked the angels to watch over my mum just after she had come out from her mastectomy. She called me and said that she had woken up to the bedroom being full with the most vibrant lights whizzing around her and lighting up the room, and that the whole room had smelled of flowers. I knew that the angels had heard my plea. She then would phone up and tell me that nearly every time she went to the hospital, a white fluffy feather would always land on her cheek or shoulder as she walked in for her treatment. I asked her if there was a bird's nest above the entrance (ever the analyst!) and she said that there was nothing above the entrance. She has now made a full recovery and has kept every feather. I had explained to her their significance, and I absolutely know that the subtle way of the feathers landing on her brought nothing but strength and comfort.

I keep angel cards and always refer to them on a regular basis with a certain question or just a request for guidance. They have never been wrong. Every question I have asked has been answered in the cards. This is the amazing thing: if I do not understand my predicament or why something is happening, I will involuntarily pull exactly the same card every day until I do understand how to go forward. Even more powerful is that I also receive angel messages online and they are the exact same message as the personal cards I have consulted at home. That happened very recently when I asked a question about my future career and a big decision I had to make. I not only pulled the same card three days running, but the same message for three days running was sent to my e-mail! I was then told in my head to look for the blue angel as a sign to know I was making the right decision. A couple of days after this, I stopped in the street and felt that I had to look at a shop window. In the window was a four-foot blue angel lit up! The angel was there to promote a book, but to me it was my sign!

Don't get me wrong, I'm not a guru; I am not anyone who professes to have a direct line to the angels, but I have surrendered my doubt, accepted their loving presence and I honour the fact that they are there to guide and love me during the good and bad times. You don't need to be an expert in angels and know which one does what. I have never studied them or read up on them; I just know they are there and that certain angels visit for whatever problem you have in your life.

At the beginning of 2010, again I did a review of my life and how I could project myself more to help educate the public about angels and the spirit world. Again I felt worn out. I had been travelling the country and Europe demonstrating my gift, but realized it was getting harder doing everything on my own. I needed support and someone to help me, as demand for me was becoming overwhelming and I didn't have the finance or the support to reach bigger audiences. So at the beginning of February I asked the angels if they could help me. I said that I understood if the time wasn't right, but if it was, to bring me the assistance that I needed. Within days, Mr Colin Fry, the icon of modern-day mediumship, contacted me. He had managed to see a couple of episodes of *Angels* and wanted to help me reach the public in a bigger way. I am now managed by Colin and look forward to my future.

You will always have frustrating times in your life; you will laugh, cry, scream, grieve, celebrate and learn. But do you know what? You will always have the angels there by your side if you let them. Just surrender, accept and embrace your angels with love, welcome them into your lives and you will notice the difference, I promise you.

– Nicky Alan

MOST IMPORTANT FACT

The more you can change your energy toward positivity, the more people will change in their reaction to you. People enjoy being around positive, cheerful people and once you are one, you'll find your popularity will soar, with people as well as with angels.

Recommended Reading

Lorna Byrne, *Angels in My Hair* (Arrow)

Gwynne H. Davies, *Allergies: Break Through to Health* (Capall Bann Publishing)

Sonia Ducie, *Thorsons First Directions: Numerology* (Thorsons)

Jacky Newcomb, *An Angel Held My Hand* (Harper Element)

Doreen Virtue, *How to Hear Your Angels* (Hay House)

Madeleine Walker, *An Exchange of Love* (O Books)

Danny Wallace, *Random Acts of Kindness* (Ebury Press)

Dr Roger Woolger, *Other Lives, Other Selves* (Thorsons)

Resources

http://www.jackynewcomb.com/
– the Angel Lady

http://www.supernaturalangels.org.uk

http://www.julieangelguest.co.uk/

http://www.elisewardle.co.uk
– Elise Wardle

http://www.gypsymaggierose.com
– Maggie

http://www.anexchangeoflove.com
– animal communication and healing

http://www.rosereiki.com
– healing

http://labyrinthlocator.com/
– for locating labyrinths

http://www.janetrussellpresents.com/

http://www.uoguelph.ca/atguelph/08-11-19/featuresblossom.shtml
– can plants count?

www.rachelkeene.net

http://degby.wetpaint.com/
– Diane Egby

http://www.animalsheal.co.uk
– Lynne Statham

http://www.distancehealer.net/
– Susan Grey, distance healer

www.nickyalan.co.uk
http://www.dailymail.co.uk/femail/article-1121331/
Are-angels-real-With-more-people-putting-faith-
LIZ-JONES-claims-test-.html

HEALTH ISSUES
www.cancerfungus.com
www.gwynnedavies.com

Hay House Titles of Related Interest

JOIN THE HAY HOUSE FAMILY

As the leading self-help, mind, body and spirit publisher in the UK, we'd like to welcome you to our family so that you can enjoy all the benefits our website has to offer.

 EXTRACTS from a selection of your favourite author titles

 COMPETITIONS, PRIZES & SPECIAL OFFERS Win extracts, money off, downloads and so much more

 LISTEN to a range of radio interviews and our latest audio publications

 CELEBRATE YOUR BIRTHDAY An inspiring gift will be sent your way

 LATEST NEWS Keep up with the latest news from and about our authors

 ATTEND OUR AUTHOR EVENTS Be the first to hear about our author events

 iPHONE APPS Download your favourite app for your iPhone

 HAY HOUSE INFORMATION Ask us anything, all enquiries answered

join us online at **www.hayhouse.co.uk**

 292B Kensal Road, London W10 5BE
T: 020 8962 1230 E: info@hayhouse.co.uk

ABOUT THE AUTHOR

Based in beautiful Somerset, in the UK, and happily married for 40 years, **Jenny Smedley**, DPLT, is a qualified past-life regressionist, author, TV and radio presenter and guest, international columnist and spiritual consultant, specializing in the subjects of past lives and angels. She's also an animal intuitive and tree communicator. Her own current life was turned around by a vision from one of her past lives, and problems and issues related to that life were healed and resolved in a few seconds.

Jenny has appeared on many TV shows and hundreds of radio shows, in countries including the UK, USA, Australia, New Zealand, Iceland, Tasmania, the Caribbean, South Africa and Spain.

After being shown her Master Path by an angel, Jenny was given the ability to create Mirror Angel Portraits and remote-aura pictures, and to help others connect to their angels.

www.jennysmedley.com